BORN IN THE LIFE
GENE BORRELLO
Mafia Enforcer for the Bonanno Crime Family

LOUIS ROMANO

Also By Louis Romano

Detective Vic Gonnella Series
INTERCESSION YOU THINK I'M DEAD
JUSTIFIED
THE BUTCHER OF PUNTA CANA
THE PIPELINE: TERROR FOR NEW YORK

Gino Ranno Mafia Series
FISH FARM
BESA
GAME OF PAWNS
EXCLUSION: THE FIGHT FOR CHINATOWN

Zip Code Series for Teens & Young Adults
ZIP CODE

Short Story Series
ANXIETY'S NEST
ANXIETY'S CURE
BEFORE I DROP DEAD (Things I Want to Tell You)

Heritage Collection Series and True Crime Series
CARUSI: The Shame of Sicily
John Alite; Mafia International

Acknowledgments

I want to thank Gene Borrello for the story you are about to read.

My discussions started with Gene while he was finishing his time in prison. I found his story to be compelling, so I stepped out of my comfort zone of writing fiction novels and moved into the true crime genre.

Gene and I spent many days tying together his stories, along with the research I did on the Bonanno family, for the years in which he was active in the mob.

Thank you to John Alite for his help in getting Gene and me together and for his guidance.

~Lou Romano

I want to thank my fellow prison mate for helping me get my thoughts down and author Louis Romano who has taken on my story and become a great friend and confidante.

~Gene Borrello

PROLOGUE

At this writing, I am still incarcerated awaiting sentencing. As it stands right now, my sentencing guidelines are fifteen years to life. Usually, the average reduction is fifty percent. Having cooperated against Ronnie Giallanzo and the infamous Vincent "Uncle Vin" Asaro, I am hoping my cooperation will be deemed above average by a generous judge who will set me free sooner rather than later.

My release is imminent, and I believe it will be sometime during 2019.

With that in mind, as I plan or try to plan for the next step, my thoughts turn back to the mob. Mob life, its glorification, and how it affected my life.

THE MEETING

I pointed to a tattoo the length of Gene Borrello's inner arm. 'OMERTA,' it read. The word for the Sicilian Mafia code of silence.

"I guess you didn't follow that code too closely, Gene," I blurted.

He laughed, understanding my meaning, as he had turned on 'the life' and became what many would call a rat. After hearing his story, though, it was clear Gene was no rat. He was a survivor of a life that turns on its members.

"I was always loyal to the bosses until I was facing life in prison for the crimes I did. There was no reason I should give my life away for people who ultimately screwed me good. That's why I want to tell my story."

The first time I met Gene Borrello was in a cigar lounge in Fort Lee, New Jersey. I had spoken to him several times while he was in the Federal Correctional Institution in Fairton, New Jersey. The subject was about this book. I could tell he was as intense as our mutual friend, John Alite, the famous, or infamous, Gambino mob enforcer who brokered Gene's and my meeting right smack in the middle of the COVID-19 debacle.

In spite of the quarantine with the mask-and-gloves ritual, Gene walked in, and we threw caution to the wind and shook hands. No six-foot social-distancing rule applied to either of us.

Unlike so many wiseguys I've met over the years, who

generally dress to the nines, or simply dressed well, Gene wore shorts, a t-shirt, and sneakers, but his eyes immediately reminded me of a hungry leopard, an experienced hunter on the prowl. His purpose was clear. Gene Borrello wanted to tell his story as a mob enforcer for the Bonanno crime family. I could say he was intense, but intense would be an understatement. Gene doesn't relax; he sat on the edge of a Havana Chair, his piercing brown eyes sizing me up to see if I was the real-deal writer he'd heard about.

He clearly worked out every day and was in great physical shape. His dark eyes partially hidden under a Nike baseball cap were striking. His language was pure mafia, with the nomenclature of a true wiseguy.

Borrello's story is not something everyone has already heard or read about or has seen on various documentaries and dramatic cable shows on the history of the Mafia. This story is current day, not something from the days of Bugsy Siegel, Albert Anastasia, and Meyer Lansky or a Mario Puzo compilation of the old days.

The Borrello saga is about a thirty-six-year-old mob enforcer who was born into the life with the true, nitty gritty, unglamorous street life that led to his being locked up for a third of his life, until he finally said… enough.

Enforcer for the mob. That would become Gene Borrello's title and description by state law enforcement agencies and the Federal Bureau of Investigation.

More specifically, Borrello was an enforcer for two people: Vincent "Uncle Vin" Asaro, the Bonanno consigliere, and his nephew, Ronald "Ronnie G." Giallanzo, a Mafia captain.

Uncle Vin was tall, thin, muscular, and handsome. The women, young and old, all loved him. His booming voice was always heard as he yelled at everyone, except when he had them in stitches from laughter. He was funny as hell when he was in the right mood. Uncle Vin's psychopathic behavior was what kept him alive and flourishing in the Mafia for decades.

Vinny was put on trial for the 1978 Lufthansa Heist thirty-seven years later, in 2015, by the United States Government, which has a longer memory than the Arabs, who are still pissed off about the Crusades. The government had a small army of credible informants and witnesses, wire taps, photos, and videos of Uncle Vin from the time of that famous robbery. Amazingly, and inexplicably, Vinny Asaro was acquitted by a jury of his peers. The case was so high profile that it would dominate worldwide news headlines for months. Uncle Vin was on the front page of every newspaper in New York City, and, unlike John Gotti, Asaro loathed publicity. The government's loss was devastating to them. The feds had spent millions of dollars on the investigation and prosecution of the notorious Vincent Asaro. It was a blow to the government and to the United States Attorney's Office for the Eastern District of New York.

Ronnie G was groomed as a gangster in the image of Uncle Vin, his mentor, but was notorious and wealthy in his own right. His home, a veritable mansion in Queens, N.Y., was valued in the threeto four-million-dollar range. His bookmaking and loan shark operations would make him tens of millions of dollars. More money, more power, more trappings is how the life goes.

Ronnie was short and dark with a compact build and was usually very unfriendly and disrespectful to most people.

The government, with all its resources, had no clue of the magnitude of Ronnie's worth and illegal income. Eventually, the government would do a full forensic accounting investigation and estimate Ronnie's net worth at thirty-five million dollars. Not so bad for a guy without a trade or education.

There were few gambling and shylock operations comparable to Ronnie G's in New York City; to rise to his level of success during this period in mob history was truly rare. Gene Borrello was surrounded and taught by the best.

In Gene Borrello's own words,

"My role was to oversee Ronnie's operations and anything else he needed or wanted. However, my specialty and value to Ronnie and Uncle Vin was violence. An order was given, any order whatsoever, and I would execute the order to completion. You have to realize the amount of treachery in the Mafia. The only person you could trust was yourself. I seen a guy shoot his best friend on orders from the boss."

From a simple whack across the face for a late gambling or loan sharking payment to killing a life-long friend, nothing was out of bounds for Gene. Uncle Vin and Ronny G knew that if Borrello was given an order, it was done. He allowed no questions, no negotiations, and no reprieve. Begging only made matters worse for the victim. When Borrello got his orders, the only thing he had to do was get them done and report back to Ronnie G or Vinnie Asaro.

For a period of three years when Ronnie G was in prison, Gene Borrello ran Ronnie G's entire operation and answered to Uncle Vin and only to Uncle Vin. That was an enviable position for a twenty-one-year associate in the Bonanno family. The friendship and trust would grow beyond Borrello's wildest expectations. On a daily basis, Asaro would school Borrello, telling him, "Genie, you're the future".

On one occasion, Vin needed triple bypass heart surgery.

Borrello recounts, "I went to visit him and right there in his hospital room, in walks none other than Thomas "Tommy D" DiFiore, the Bonanno Family boss. I immediately recognized him and felt a pit in my stomach. Tommy D gave Vin a questioning look, raising his eyebrows and tilting his head with a smirk on his face. Vin announced, 'You can talk, he's okay.' Uncle Vin introduced me to Tommy D. 'This is Gene, one of my guys.'

"Some guys go their entire criminal careers without even once meeting their boss. I had arrived."

GROWING UP

Having been born Gene Peter Borrello and been originally from Canarsie, Brooklyn, he first ended up in rough-and-tumble Ozone Park, Queens, with his mom after his parents split up when he was ten years old.

Gene himself then landed in Howard Beach at the impressionable age of sixteen. Howard Beach was a known Mafia stronghold. He looked up with rapt admiration to the Mafiosi. The mobsters, from soldiers to capos[1] to bosses, lived and raised their families in Howard Beach, making their livings as criminals throughout the five boroughs and beyond.

Now, not every Italian-American kid who grew up in Howard Beach looked at the wiseguys as role models for success. However, Gene Borrello did just that. He saw how these men had kept the undesirable minorities out of the neighborhood, kept the area safe, drove expensive cars, dressed well, spread the cash around, and, most importantly, how the mobsters commanded total respect.

---

[1] Mafia Capo regime

BORRELLO FAMILY HISTORY

Aside from Gene Borrello's criminal grandfather and father, his first cousin, John "Johnny Boy" Borrello, was also a Mafia associate by the time he was twenty years old. He was first around Charles Carneglia, a notorious skipper[2] with the Gambino family.

Johnny Boy had three murders under his belt by the time he was twenty-two, which took place in Fort Lauderdale, Florida. He was a mob enforcer and owned a piece of an automobile chop shop in Queens with Vinnie Asaro. Johnny Boy was an up-and-coming star and would have been straightened out at a very young age if not for Vito Guzzo.

Eddie Wrecker, along with Johnny Boy Borrello, were ordered to murder a crazy man, Vito Guzzo, who ran a Queens crime ring for the Colombo family, which had tormented the borough for years with bank robberies, home invasions, extortion, and murder.

Following their orders, Wrecker and Johnny Boy shot Guzzo six times. He was hit in this throat, his head, and his spleen...and lived. Guzzo would soon seek his revenge.

On October 9, 1996, Gene Borrello was only twelve years old when Guzzo caught up with his older cousin, Johnny Boy. Along with Anthony Tabbita, Guzzo had stolen a white District Attorney van. Johnny Boy and his gal, Lisa Sellers, a former girlfriend of Guzzo's, were sitting in

---

[2] Another name for Capo.

Johnny Boy's car when his killers found them.

Guzzo removed the screaming Lisa from the car, and he and Tabbita massacred Johnny Boy with dozens of rounds from pistols and a shotgun.

No one retaliated.

This was part of the life, and Gene Borrello learned the dangers at a young and impressionable age.

Gene grew up in a family that understood and accepted why their men spent a good part of their lives in prison. His father spent his time in Clinton prison for armed robbery. His grandfather, Frank Guerrera, drove a school bus for thirty years during the day and was a drug dealer and hijacker by night. He ultimately died inside prison doing a 5-flat bid[3] for illegal firearms. He also did a 3-9 for coke dealing where he took most of the heat for his grandson, Gene Borrello.

Gene describes his family, detailing his words in quick bursts of facts:

"To my mother's good fortune, she met Frank, who was the opposite of my father. My father was insane, but I was closest to my grandfather. We just clicked."

Gene 'clicked' with a man who was implicated in the murder of Tony "The Hat" Cornero way back when their relative, Anthony "Fat Andy" Ruggiano, was a powerhouse. It seemed Tony and Grandpa Borrello got into an argument about money. Tony, a made man, came

---

[3] Jail sentence. Usually prison time.

up dead the next day, and the money was gone. It didn't look too good for grandpa.

Killing a made man is a death sentence in the Mafia life. There is no twelve-person jury that would find guilt beyond a reasonable doubt. The mob would do their own investigation, make a decision, and the body of the accused may or may not be found. If found, it very well could be whole or in pieces. It was that simple.

Enter "Fat Andy" Ruggiano, Gene's grandfather's brotherin-law and his mother's uncle, who sequestered grandpa at a safe place in upstate New York. Ruggiano convinced his colleagues that Grandpa Guerrera was not a killer, and the old man was saved from the inevitable hit.

Gene goes on to highlight the life of his great-uncle Fat Andy with a gleam in his eyes:

"Fat Andy came up through the ranks from being one of seven of Albert Anastasia's bodyguards. When Anastasia was shot dead in a barber chair in Manhattan in 1958, the order went out that all seven of "The Mad Hatter's" bodyguards were to be clipped. Fat Andy and Tony Lee, a confidant of Ruggiano, got a pass from Don Carlo Gambino himself. Ruggiano would become a capo, a skipper, in the Gambino family, running the entire Queens operations. John Gotti worked for Ruggiano in his early days in the family. With nearly fifty murders under his belt, Fat Andy was Mafia royalty."

At a family gathering when he was thirteen, Gene Borrello remembers seeing the celebrated Fat Andy:

"At that moment, I wanted that life. I wanted the money,

the respect, and the power. School wasn't for me. The mob was!"

Growing up and being raised around mostly Gambino associates or members like his uncle, Fat Andy Ruggiano, and his cousin, Johnny Boy Borrello, Gene was now on the fast track to becoming a real gangster. By bloodline, Borrello should have been with the Gambino family, but he was with his good friend Bobby G and drifted to the Bonanno family. Officially, he was a Bonanno associate under Ronnie Giallanzo. To be an associate of a wiseguy means Borrello couldn't tie his own shoes without going through Ronnie. Ronnie was totally responsible for Gene- good, bad or otherwise.

Everything Borrello did would reflect on Ronnie G. Borrello was 'with him.'

"This term can mean death," Borrello explains. "For instance, let's say I was to sleep with a woman I picked up at a nightclub. We both had a few drinks, and I take her to my apartment, and we sleep together. My friend Ronnie Manns walks in on us in the middle of sex, and screams, 'Gene, I need to talk to you right now.' Hearing the urgency in his voice, I jump up, the hell with the girl. I think it is related to our criminal life, but when we are outside the bedroom, Ronnie tells me, 'Gene what the fuck are you doing? That's so-and-so's wife.' Well, so-and-so is a highly respected made guy serving 5-15 in Clinton state penitentiary for attempted murder. Should 'so-and-so' find out, I could be clipped. Either by Ronnie G or another family."

Because Borrello was an associate, he was supposed to

know better. Ignorance of the rules of the Mafia was no excuse to break them. This was one of the reasons that it could take years for an associate to be proposed for membership. There were many rules an associate had to learn to navigate life in the La Cosa Nostra. Sleeping with a made-guy's wife was a big no-no, punishable by death.

From the time he was released from Rikers Island County Jail in 2004, Gene had partnered up with Bobby G, Ronnie's nephew, prior to being put on record as an associate. They would hang out with Ronnie G and several other made guys and associates.

Hanging around these guys, Borrello picked up tidbits of wisdom about the "life" that could perhaps save his life. Sometimes Ronnie G or one of the guys would offer a lesson, or there would be a teachable moment."Though it was not spoken of, they know as well as me and Bobby G knew, we were the future of this outfit along with some of the other guys my age or a bit older. We were the next wave of button[4] men to vie for money, control, and power within the structure of the Bonanno crime family," Gene recalled.

Being Ronnie's nephew, Bobby G was automatically on record. He was no civilian, and he was an aspiring gangster just like Gene.

Bobby G was being fast-tracked because of his family ties. "Bobby G's uncle is Ronnie G, one of the wealthiest, toughest, and most feared gangsters in Howard Beach. But Bobby G's great uncle, Vincent 'Uncle Vin' Asaro, may be

---

[4] Credential as a made-man. Generally untouchable

the most infamous gangster alive in 2018," Gene explained.

Gene and Bobby, now with Ronnie G, were reined in from their prior cowboy escapades, but life would not be any less risky or boring. Ronnie G would teach Gene and Bobby G his business dealings and how they would fit into his criminal empire. Gene explains, "We were part of his inner crew comprised of both made guys and associates. In the structure of organized crime, a made guy is a soldier, and all soldiers are equal. A soldier answers to his captain. Captains answer to the hierarchy, the counselor or consigliere, the number three in the organization, the under boss, and the boss."

Ronnie G at that time was not a captain, yet three other soldiers would answer to Ronnie.

Gene goes on, "You see, while they were equal in the La Cosa Nostra, Ronnie's criminal empire yielded millions, and his fellow soldiers earned for and from him. Ronnie's inner circle comprised of three soldiers and seven associates. The outer circle of associates was approximately ten. But this number is deceiving because an associate can be anyone that has any kind of tie to Ronnie G. Based on that, the number would be in the hundreds."

Any Bonanno associate under or with Ronnie Giallanzo would have to learn how Ronnie G wanted things done, or else. He had peculiar quirks and a bad temper, and that was that.

Ronnie G's Early Years

"Like Bobby G and I coming up together, Ronnie G's partner was Mike Padavona. Just like us, they began as friends: robbing, fighting, burglaries, and only God knows what else. They would become associates in the mob together. I think they were both brought in by Uncle Vin. The two of them were proposed to become made members of the La Cosa Nostra, but for Padavona, there would be a bad sequence of events.

"I was around when things went wrong, and I had the opportunity to hear it from Mike Padavona first hand. Mike had explained to me he and Ronnie were to be 'made' at the same time in 1994. Mike had a run in with Peter Gotti, Don Gotti's youngest son. Gotti with a gun. The Gotti kid was not an associate, just exploiting his father's name, running wild, doing what he wanted. Because he was the son of a Mafia don, Padavona didn't want to act on his own to exact revenge. Padavona went to Uncle Vin to let him know what happened and to get permission to kill Gotti. Uncle Vin said, 'Get him.' You see, what the Gotti kid did, even though Padavona was an associate under Uncle Vin, was a death sentence. Gotti was not an associate or made member of any family. He had to pay. When Vin said 'get him,' he had stipulated that Padavona had twenty-four hours to do the piece of work; after that, it's done. Had they killed Gotti during that time, Uncle Vin could argue the Gotti kid knew who Padavona was and knew he was with Vin.

"During this time, Peter Gotti was running wild, doing whatever he wanted with no regard for anyone. He was

14

riding on his father's reputation, but Peter was a tough guy in his own right. After the incident with Padavona, Gotti would have told his father (the boss) what happened in the event of blowback from Padavona and Uncle Vin.

"Remember, Uncle Vin was a notorious and extremely dangerous gangster, reputed to have killed a bunch of people. The clock was ticking. Ronnie G and Padavona were both hunting Peter Gotti. Had they found him, they would have killed him. But, once the time passed, the administration of the La Cosa Nostra would get involved. The incident would be squashed. And it was. Padavona was furious. Later, Padavona had told Uncle Vin he was still going to get Gotti. Uncle Vin told Padavona, 'No you're not.' Padavona insisted on getting Gotti, but Vin told him the stipulation had expired. Mike persisted.

"Padavona had an argument with Vin over this, and it ended his criminal career with the Bonanno crime family. Padavona would take up with another crime family, but Vin would not release him, so Mike could not become a made member of another family. Years later, Padavona would come back to the Bonanno family and become a made member in 2011.

"Ronnie G was a street kid turned gangster. At one time, he had a union job. It would turn out Ronnie would work on the World Trade Center after the Towers were struck September 11, 2001. For being on site and clearing the debris, later found to contain asbestos, years later, Ronnie would receive a check in excess of one-hundred thousand dollars sbestos damage to his lungs.

"But before that period, Ronnie G was struggling

financially. I guess it was around the late nineties. He was making money that was illegal in two ways: he was breaking federal law and La Cosa Nostra's rules by providing 'protection' to drug dealers. You see, according to mob rules, made members cannot deal drugs, cannot provide protection, cannot in any way, shape, or form have anything to do with the sale of illegal drugs. The reason being is that it is much too easy to get arrested and prosecuted for drug conspiracies by the state and federal governments.

"While this may be against the 'rules,' many wiseguys make money in the drug business. Ronnie G is a perfect example. Down to his last twenty-thousand in the nineties, he began providing protection to drug dealers through an associate, Mike Palmaccio.

"Palmaccio was a drug dealer, a big drug dealer, several wiseguys (other than Bonanno's) were trying to shake Palmaccio down, but Mike wouldn't pay. Mike wasn't brave, he was cheap. He was also hard headed on paying protection to Gambino members. They, the Gambinos, were so pissed at Palmaccio that they were hunting him to kill him. Palmaccio was giving them the run around the whole time until he got with Ronnie G.

"With Ronnie G needing an influx of cash and Palmaccio needing protection, Ronnie put his arm around Mike; it was a winwin situation. Now, with Ronnie in the picture, the Gambino mob had to back off.

"Palmaccio wasn't just dealing drugs, he was providing other dealers with their supply, and these lower level dealers were paying Ronnie G through Palmaccio for protection. 'Protection,' meaning should any others attempt to extort money from these dealers, they say, 'I'm with Ronnie G,' and that should cause enough fear to make the venture too risky, for now, you were trying to shake down the mob.

"These guys were paying protection for nothing. Had anyone reached out for Ronnie G, there was not a damn thing he could do. Remember, he wasn't permitted to make money from drugs. It was nothing but a ruse, a hustle.

"This venture and hooking up with Mike Palmaccio was the beginning of a fruitful operation that would lead each of them to make millions of dollars.

"Palmaccio, not the violent type, was known in mob parlance as an earner, a guy with a knack for making money. Ronnie G took Mike in as an associate and would school him on how to conduct himself as a mobster, and after several years, Ronnie G would 'put him up,' or propose him to be straightened out. Palmaccio became a made member of the Bonanno crime family in 2002. Ronnie G would say it was the biggest mistake he ever made because Palmaccio simply was not, at his core, a gangster.

"Palmaccio would allow people to walk all over him. He was an earner who bought his button and was an embarrassment to Ronnie G and the Bonanno family.

"Palmaccio was just a fuck up, there is no other way to put it. At one point, he sent out a picture on Instagram posing shirtless for women trolling for hookups. Keep in mind, this is a wiseguy. There is supposed to be some discretion, a code of conduct of proper attire and class. Mike threw that right out the window.

"John 'Bazoo' Ragano, a made guy recently released from prison and an old school gangster, somehow came across Palmaccio's picture on Instagram. Ragano enlarged the picture to eight and a half by eleven inches and brought it to Palmaccio's captain, Jerry Asaro. You would think Mike was going for a modeling job the way Ragano presented the picture to Jerry. Jerry blew a gasket and told Uncle Vin what happened.

"Vin's response was a no-brainer. The offense (posing in a way that disgraced the family) warranted death. Jerry, Vin's son, suggested mercy, but there was a twist.

"Mike Palmaccio received a call from Bazoo that instructed him to go to Bam's garage late one night, midnight. Mike knew he fucked up big this time. He called me to his house to tell me, 'They just sent for me.' Mike was trying to find out if I heard anything because he knew how close I was to Ronnie G. He asked point blank, 'You think they're gonna kill me?' I told him, 'I don't know nothing, but if you see Andrew Curro in there, run.' Curro was a known killer in the Bonanno family.

"When Mike got to the garage late that night, the streets were dead. He parked. Walking to the garage was the longest walk of his life. Once he entered, scared to death, he was verbally abused, told he was an embarrassment, and slapped by Jerry Asaro. Worst of all, they put Mike on the shelf.

"A made guy being put on the shelf is one step up from death. It is the ultimate disgrace for a gangster. Not only are you disgraced, for all intents and purposes, you are no longer Mafia. You don't report in to your boss or guy, and you are out of the loop. But Palmaccio got to live. Had Joe Massino been running the family, Palmaccio would have been dead within twenty-four hours. Palmaccio would get taken off the shelf after a year and resume the life of a gangster.

"A big factor for Palmaccio not being killed was the fact that he was an earner. The money Mike had made in the past saved him, and there would be more for him to make in the future...much more. But it's not always the potential to earn that is valuable, it's the ability to see the potential to earn in others.

"Palmaccio, eager to make up for his past embarrassment to Ronnie G, had grown up with a guy named Vincent Rossetti and saw an opportunity. Palmaccio knew his friend had a fascination with the Mafia. Vincent had become a broker on Wall Street being in a prime spot.

"The point being, because of the stories, lore, mystique surrounding the mob, people are affected in a couple of ways. Some are repulsed by the crime, violence, and see Mafioso as parasites sucking the life from civil society. The others are the complete opposite: intrigued, fascinated, dream of what types of criminals they would be. They were enamored with the 'life:' the trappings of wealth, power, and all that comes with it. Pulling up to the hottest nightclub in Manhattan, you, your girlfriend, your pal, and his girl, with the line going around the block, greet the doorman, discretely hand him some cash, and walk right in. Not because you are some big business executive or some other V.I.P., but because you're a gangster. You move to the front of the line because you are feared. Vinny Rossetti wanted in this life, and he would do so through Mike Palmaccio. Mike, in turn, would realize the potential of putting Rossetti and Ronny G together.

"Rosetti would go as far as telling Palmaccio he could make big money. Palmaccio's eyes lit up, he had one on the hook for Ronnie.

"Palmaccio would introduce Rosetti to Ronny G, and Ronnie would play the role of the gangster that he was. Ronnie would talk of what he and his connections could and would do for Rosetti. At one point, Ronny G went with Palmaccio to another brokerage firm and beat up the broker, hitting him with the phone to get the list or his client book. They got the book.

"That was it, the hook was set. Rossetti wound up paying Ronnie fiftyto one-hundred thousand dollars a month to kick up to him."

"Think about that for a minute, six-hundred thousand to one point two million dollars a year for protection? Protection from what, the boogeyman? For that kind of money, he could have hired a team of mercenaries, licensed to carry guns. Actually, he could have hired retired SEAL team members. He could have hired the guy who shot Bin Laden and still had tens of thousands remaining.

"Ronnie was telling Rossetti the whole time, 'You' re gonna be straightened out.' He never had any intention of proposing Vinny Rossetti to become a made member of the Mafia.

"Ronnie was furious. Even after he chased Vinny, he had me go torch the wife's car and her father's car. The cars were burnt to a crisp, totaled.

"More was to come. The book was not closed with Vinny Rossetti yet. Ronnie G would be indicted for extortion of a stock market firm. Vinny Rossetti would wear a recording device when he met Ronnie, who was out on bail. Ronnie's bail was revoked, and he was put behind bars. Ronnie G would plead out and receive a sentence of seven-and-a-half years. He would be sent to prison in November, 2006.

CUTTING HIS TEETH

Grandpa Guerrera and eighteen-year-old Gene were pinched together on a narcotics bust. Being the stand-up guy that he was, the old man took the heavy sentence, and Genie was left with only eighteen months.

"The old timers really liked it when you did jail time. It was good for your character and your career," Gene blurted. "I was looking for a spot in the life, and they heard about me doing stickups all over Queens, robbing jewelry stores, commercial robbery stuff."

Fresh out jail for the narcotics, Gene was anxious to get his chance to be in the life. With the help of a Gambino associate called Hootie, Gene started selling some coke, Vicodin, and any other prescription meds popular at the time. With a few cooperative doctors and pharmacy robberies, the cash started to flow.

Gene started cutting his teeth doing illegal activities on a daily basis. That was his job.

With his good friend Bobby G, nephew of the Bonanno skipper "Ronnie G" Giallanzo, Gene scored on a jewelry store heist, pulling in seven-hundred-and-fifty thousand dollars-worth of merchandise. Because they were young and dumb, their fence, Vito, gave them a mere forty thousand for the boys to share. As time passed and more goods were stolen, Gene found he could do much better fencing jewelry among the Orthodox Jews in the 47th Street Diamond District in Manhattan. Gene began to spread his wings, robbing anything and everything that was in his sight.

Ronnie G's radar screen picked up on Gene and Bobby G's work and brought them into the Bonanno clan. Gene got his chance as an associate.

Acting on a tip, Bobby G and Gene learned of a card game in the Malba section of Whitestone, Queens. Malba was an affluent area, mostly Italian families, that sat between the Whitestone and Throgs Neck Bridges near the East River. From the tip, the boys knew that the game was a Gambino family spot and that their mark was a Gambino capo who wore an eighty-thousand-dollar Rolex watch and who would be leaving the game flush with cash. The game was owned by mobster Al Trucchio's associate and one of the sons of the infamous Gotti capo, "Quack Quack" Ruggiero. Very serious people, to say the least. It would seem that the club and the game were protected.

The mark was an owner of a few nightclubs, including Cavo, obviously another Gambino source of large, steady income.

Gene and Bobby G waited in a car outside the card game. It was one o'clock in the morning.

"How the fuck long is this game?" Gene asked.

"It's over when it's over. You gotta learn some patience, Genie," Bobby G replied, his eyes steadily glaring at the front door of the club.

Gene repeated the plan.

"You stay inside the car. I'll snatch the goods, and we are outta here in a minute."

"You gonna shoot him?" Bobby G asked. He kept repeating, "Don't shoot him."

"Don't be stupid. A shot will bring the other players onto the street, and then we are totally fucked," Gene instructed.

At four A.M., out walks the Gambino associate, known to both Gene and Bobby G. Suddenly, Borrello fearlessly jumped out of the car, his face covered by a ski mask and his head topped with a baseball cap pulled low over his brow.

Gene smashed his pistol onto the back of the associate's head, sending him reeling to the pavement.

"Gimmie the money and that fucking watch," Gene commanded.

"Please don't kill me," the mark pleaded. But he wouldn't give up the Rolex.

Two more whacks with the gun onto the mark's head, who was now in tears.

"I swear I'll blow your fucking head off. The watch...now!"

Gene got the watch and a bag of money and fled the scene as planned.

Genie and Bobby G's activity was a death sentence if they were caught. First, they robbed a Gambino member at a protected card game, and second Gene pistol whipped the guy. In that life, you strike a crew member, even a hand slap to the face, and you die.

Mafia rules 101. Gene and Bobby G pretended they didn't get the memo.

Gene and Bobby G were in a state of celebration. What a score! They split the fifty grand that was in the bag. Gene took the Rolex to be fenced at a later date. They estimated they could get a minimum of forty-thousand from the Diamond District contact. A forty-five-grand score for each of them. No kick up to Ronnie G, who was totally unaware of this stick up. Another big no-no.

At ten o'clock that next morning, Gene's doorbell rang. It was Ronnie G and one of his crew, Mike Padavona, his major earner,

a.k.a. 'Mikey Boats.'

"Hey, Ronnie, what's up?" Gene asked. He knew by the ferocious look on Ronnie's face that Ronnie G hadn't stopped by for a cup of black coffee.

"You worked last night?" Ronnie seethed. "Yeah."

"What did you do? Don't fucking lie to me."

"A stick up in Whitestone, no big deal. I was gonna square with you later," Gene replied. His asshole tightened up.

Ronnie ordered, 'Turn around, go upstairs, and bring me that fuckin' watch and the money. All of it."

"Ronnie…"

"Turn around, go upstairs, and bring me the watch and

the money," Ronnie repeated. He was speaking through his clenched jaw.

Borrello brought the goods as ordered. "Is this all the money, Genie?" "Ah…no. It's half."

"Where the fuck is the other half, you cocksucker?" "Bobby G has it."

"I know my nephew was with you. His brother told me. " "Yeah."

"Are you fucking kidding me or what, you stupid fuck? Do you know who you robbed? He's a Gambino."

"No way! We had no idea," Gene lied. His acting wasn't too good.

"Bullshit. You stay put until I send for you and that asshole nephew of mine. Understood? I don't know if I can save you two."

Later that day, Ronnie G sent for[5] Gene and Bobby G. They brought along Richie Boy, who gave the boys the score to begin with, and who rolled over on them to Ronnie G. Bobby G's older brother, Richie Boy, was the best friend of Gambino member Jamie Ruggiero, also a man of respect thorough his Mafia family.

"You fuckin' guys may not see your twenty-first birthdays. We have a sit-down tonight with the Gambinos. You, Genie Boy, will hand the stuff to them. You, other

[5] When an associate, soldier or made man is called in by their boss. They could be killed for an infraction or killed if they didn't show up when called for.

moron, how the fuck do you rob an associate? You been around the life since you were a baby.

Don't tell me you didn't know what you were doing, you dumb fuck."

Bobby G swallowed hard. "I swear to God. We had no idea.

We're sorry!"

"Sorry, oh okay, I'll just tell them you are both retarded and you are sorry. You will pray a rosary and that's that. Get the fuck out of here with that bullshit! I don't know if I can get you a pass here. I doubt it…I seriously doubt it.

Ronnie went on to abuse his nephew for a good half-hour. Gene kept his mouth shut and his eyes looking straight forward. He didn't want to show any fear. They didn't know who they robbed.

That was their story, and they were clinging to it for their lives.

They stayed in Ronnie's club until it was time to go to Brooklyn. One of Ronnie's guys drove. Ronnie sat in the shotgun seat. Gene, Bobby G, and Richie Boy sat in the back seat. They rode in silence.

Gene said later, "I figured they wouldn't clip us with Bobby G there, but I wasn't really sure. They could have just taken me. I wasn't family.

In the basement of the darkened funeral home on 86th Street in Brooklyn, three Gambino members and one capo met Ronnie and the rest of the crew.

Ronnie started the meeting, "Look, these guys are fucking cowboys. They had no idea who they were fucking with."

"Ronnie, they work for you?" the capo inquired. "They do." "Then maybe I have to think you sent them to rob us, no?"

"Like I said, they are cowboys. I had no idea it was them until I got the call this morning. My gut told me it was them. On my word, I, or anyone with me, had no idea. That would be insanity.

Our families get along on everything. C'mon, why would you even suspect me? You guys know me my whole life, for Christ's sake."

Ronnie looked sharply at Gene, who wordlessly handed a bag with the money and the Rolex to the Gambino capo.

Ronnie uttered, "If you want to tax us, tax us. But this was just two young and stupid assholes trying to look good."

"So, they knew exactly where to go and rob us?" the capo asked.

"Everyone on the street knew there was a big game in Whitestone. Not everyone, especially these two morons, knew it was yours," Ronnie stated.

"Only one reason they get a pass on this. First off, you did the right thing, Ronnie, and brought the stuff back. After that, we know this kid's family, so out of respect to Fat Andy, they get a pass this one time. Ronnie, you need to keep your people under control. You know our rules. You're responsible for them. Cowboys don't work in this thing."

After they left, while driving back in the car, Ronnie warned Gene and Bobby G. No more stick ups until he cleared the work.

The next screw up, and everyone could go. Gene had to thank his uncle for his life.

Lesson learned…right?

Nope. In spite of the sit-down in the funeral home basement that could have gone very badly, and in spite of Ronnie G's warning, three months later, Gene and Bobby G were at it again.

This time, they heard that Genovese capo Allie Shades traveled from his social club to his home and was always loaded with a briefcase full of cash. Gene and Bobby G cased Allie Shades for a few days, and then they made their move. On the night of the robbery, Allie Shades pulled into the narrow driveway at his red-brick home in Brooklyn.

Thinking he was about to be hit when a masked gunman opened his car door, Allie began blaring the car's horn. Allie Shades fought all the way once he realized it wasn't a hit but just a robbery. Gene cracked him with his pistol. "You motherfucker!" Shades screamed.

Gene later would tell the rest of the story. "I was about to shoot him in the groin and take the cash when I heard a woman screaming. It was Allie's wife. She came out on the porch screaming and cursing. She had a shotgun and waved it around. I fired two shots at her and missed."

Gene ran to the car, and Bobby G took off. Cowboys? Or self-destructive mental cases?

Allie Shades never gave up the money.

In 2014, Gene Borrello was no stranger to Rikers Island. He knew as he approached the jail entrance in the Steinway neighborhood of Queens and took the forty-two-hundred-foot girder bridge to the jail compound, he would likely not be going home after he was sentenced to prison, at least until he was an old man.

Before his first bid in state prison, Borrello did a total of forty-seven months, on and off in arguably the worst jail in the United States. Most prisoners were held at Rikers for a year or less as they awaited trial or sentencing to state prison. The maximum number of prisoners on Rikers was nine thousand. When Borrello was serving time for various crimes he committed, there were over fourteen thousand inmates.

God damn, fuck, he thought, as he sat in his cell awaiting a visit from his attorney. This time, he was charged with multiple crimes. Extortion, home invasions, burglary, conspiracy in New York, armed robbery in Florida, and state conspiracy. A major federal indictment was also pending. Gene was screwed

As he sat on the edge of his bed in his black, Nike t-shirt, a pair of black, below-the-knee Nike shorts, and a pair of white, Jordan, high-top sneakers, hands in his face, the noise and clatter of the other cellmates in the maximum security, C-95, 8 Upper cell block did not distract him from his thoughts.

I am so fucking screwed this time, he thought. C-95, 8 Upper cell-block on Rikers Island meant you had got nothing to lose. This was the worst cell-block in all of the hell hole that was Rikers Island.

Going to jail and eventually to prison was an expected inevitability in the life. Not many Mafia members can say they were never locked up or did a bid for offenses from racketeering to murder.

How a man did his time measures him in La Cosa Nostra.

Did he align himself with the right people? Did he fight his way out of situations when he had to, or did he chirp like a bird to the FBI to lighten his time?

Mostly, until he himself was turned on by the mob, Gene Borrello was a stand-up guy.

Because of his propensity to violence, Borrello was not held in a dormitory of sixty-eight prisoners at Rikers. Instead, he found himself in a max-house of thirty maniacs and wolves, where he was forced to keep his wits about him twenty-four-seven.

Mostly, he was the only white guy at the C-95 cell-block population, where his reputation as a Mafia member gave him instant respect among the members of the Bloods and the Latin Kings. They loved Gino, as they called him, probably to make him sound more Italian. These gangs fought amongst each other inside Rikers, and their beefs often turned into retribution both inside the jail and on the streets. If there was a skirmish in the cell-block, word got out onto the neighborhoods through visitors, eventually leading to shootings, stabbings, and murder on the streets of New York City.

Borrello's reputation as a violent maniac who would fearlessly stand up to anyone kept the wolves at bay for the most part. He was known to be good with his hands and even better with a shiv.

The Bloods especially respected Borrello because some of them had done work with Gino on the outside. They also read about his work in the newspapers and various mob blogs and crime websites. That respect got him his own table, where he held court on a daily basis.

Gino was in charge of the 550s,[6] neutral prisoners who were not affiliated with gang bangers. His presence protected these men who would otherwise fall as easy prey to the Latin Kings and the Bloods.

On one particular day, Borrello got word that a guy named Dino from Bayside, Queens, would be brought to C-95. Dino, a diminutive Italian whose five foot, six inch body had been ravaged and depleted by his drug addiction, had messed up in a drug program and was misplaced in this cell-block. He had no violent crimes or any other record that deserved the maximum-security attention.

Borrello took Dino under his wing with the other 550s and protected him.

---

[6] A person in jail with no mob affiliation. E.g. Latin King, Aryan Nation Mafia, Bloods etc.

Prior to Dino's first day, there were two Latin Kings: K.O. and Excalibur. Gino and Excalibur didn't get along very well, starting out when they first met inside C-95.

Both K.O. and Excalibur were short Puerto Ricans who had chiseled muscles, which they both showed off under their white wife-beater t-shirts. K.O.'s head was shaved bald. Excalibur wore his jet-black hair just above his olive-toned shoulders.

"What's your name, bro?" Gene had asked him.

"Excalibur."

"Say again?"

"Bro, my name is Excalibur!"

"I ain't calling you that fucked up name, bro, what's your real name?"

"Excalibur," the inmate yelled. He flexed his muscles to reveal a colorful sword tattoo the length of his arm.

"Okay, I'll call you EX." Not a very good start.

Dino's family took care of him with money for the commissary where he could buy snacks, cold-cuts, soda, and candy to augment the horrible food which was served. The difference between C-95 inmates and others inside Rikers is that max security inmates were not permitted to go to the commissary to shop. The goods were brought into C-95 in a rolling cart by the C.O.s,[7] the cops of Rikers. Dino would get one hundred and fifty

---

[7] Correctional Officers aka jail guards aka cops.

dollars put into his account by his family. Most of the inmates at C-95 got nothing or next to nothing from the outside. Dino was a mark.

On this one particular day, Borrello had been brought down to see his visiting mother and brother, leaving Dino exposed to K.O. and Excalibur. The two Latin Kings beat him up pretty badly, messing up his face and taking his commissary items from his ten by ten, blue-gray painted, one-man cell. Dino was locked inside his cell when his assailants left.

Dino was a 550 and a herb, a harmless guy who was more like a nerd than a criminal.

When Borrello returned to C-95, the Bloods told him to look inside Dino's cell. Gino saw the bloody mess that was once Dino's face. Dino's blood had flowed down from his broken nose and soaked most of his light gray gym shirt.

The Bloods warned K.O. and Excalibur that Gino would be pissed. "He ain't no regular white kid. He a maniac!"

The C.O.s also respected Borrello as a Bonanno member. "Yo, open this cell," Borrello demanded.

"No trouble, Gino," the guard ordered. "Fuck that, just open the cell." Borrello got the information on the beat-down from Dino. Gino went quiet instead of ballistic.

"No problem. They fight one-on-one. That's how we're going to handle this shit," Borrello commanded. He chased the C.O., who knew better than to get involved.

Excalibur was summoned, and Dino had to square up in

the main cell area with the Latin King. It seemed that K.O. and Excalibur didn't get the clear message that Borrello was a dangerous fuck and not to mess with his 550s.

Dino and Excalibur got into it. Twenty of the C-95 prisoners surrounded the two fighters to encourage the battle. After a few minutes, Borrello, his temper getting the best of him, and seeing Dino beginning to get his ass kicked, jumped into the fracas. Borrello took a shiv from his shorts that he had hidden.

Borrello punched Excalibur hard on his jaw, sending him down to the concrete floor. Borrello moved quickly, ferociously jumping on his victim. Excalibur was no match for the much taller, much stronger mob enforcer. Attempting to stick his shiv into the Latin King's face, Excalibur screamed for the C.O. while holding Borrello's arm with the shiv just inches from his face. The Bloods were screaming for Borrello to waste Excalibur when the C.O. suddenly appeared and maced Borrello in his face.

The mace did its job, burning Borrello's eyes and getting into his mouth. Borrello could hardly breathe, and Excalibur was dragged away in cuffs.

The Bloods didn't allow "oppression" within the jail. Harmless people like Dino and the other 550s were not to be beaten or robbed. Excalibur and K.O. were marked men.

Smiley, a tall, athletically built Blood member, removed Borrello's shiv and hid it. Other Bloods came to Borrello's aid, pouring milk on his face to dilute the effects of the mace. As the milk ran down his neck and onto his t-shirt, the burning liquid made Borrello wince in pain. He quickly pulled his tee off as he tried to ease the burning.

A few minutes later, the C.O. returned to Borrello. "Gino, I'm really sorry, man." "In my fucking face, dude?" Borrello hollered.

"What was I supposed to do? You were about to kill the fuckin' guy, I had to stop you. Now I have to give you a fighting ticket."

"Do what you gotta do. It'll take them six-months to put me in the hole. I'll add it to my three other tickets. By that time, I'll be locked up in fucking prison," Borrello blurted. He would have received thirtyto ninety-days punishment in solitary confinement for his jumping into the fight.

That week, K.O. was taken care of by his own Latin Kings for standing there and not helping Excalibur during the fight. They cut him from his bald head to his chin with an 11, a surgical scalpel that someone had bought from a C.O. K.O. was shunned, chased[8] from the gang by the Latin Kings, and put into PC, protective custody, with his eighty stitches.

Excalibur wasn't seen in C-95 again.

A month later, a Rikers friend of Borrello's, Sherman Manning, ran into a serious problem. Sherman, also known as Mitts because of his extremely large hands, was adopted as a child by an Italian family and hung around all Italian guys in his Queens neighborhood. He talked like a white guy and used a lot of the mob lingo, which

---

[8] Sending someone away from the life.

endeared him to Borrello. Mitts did a robbery for Gene a while back, so they had some history.

Mitts got into a beef with another black inmate. R.A., who was six-foot-six and all muscle on his massive, two-hundred-andfifty-pound body. R.A.'s biceps bulged out from his sleeveless, black sweatshirt, which was cut down to expose a rippled six-pack. He looked like he was a competitor for Mr. Universe. Mitts and R.A. didn't like each other from jump.

R.A. had sent another prisoner, a regular prisoner, not a Blood member, to cold-cock Mitts, splitting his lip open.

Borrello got word that R.A. was behind the assault, and he decided to bash a chair over R.A.'s head and shoulders during a meal time. Not the smartest move Gene ever made, but in Rikers, you couldn't let anyone get away with anything. If Gene let it go, it would signal weakness and rear.

Borrello and R.A. were separated by the C.O.s and locked in their individual cells, but not before R.A. ran up on Borrello's cell.

"I swear, I'm going to kill you, motherfucker. You as good as dead," R.A. screamed. The veins in his neck and head were swollen with anger.

"Fuck you. Bring an army, cocksucker." Borrello backed down from no one, but he knew this monster would take him apart and likely kill him.

Borrello's heart was racing in his chest. He knew that when things quieted down, he was in for it. He put the word out.

"I need something," Borrello told Smiley.

Mitts brought Borrello a shiv, unlikely the same one Gene had attempted to use on Excalibur. Shivs were used once and destroyed. Borrello was armed but knew that R.A. would likely have his own weapon. R.A. with a weapon was a nightmarish thought.

The Bloods called for a one-on-one. R.A. versus Borrello. The battle was to take place the next morning in the shower. A dozen shower heads and a white tiled floor would be the battlefield. Nobody was taking a shower early this morning.

The cells were all opened simultaneously, and Borrello went, with the shiv under his t-shirt, into the shower room to await his fate. Borrello knew he had no chance against the formidable R.A. Gene envisioned his own blood running down onto the white tiles and into the drain.

R.A. walked into the shower room with a fierce look of hatred etched on his face. Gene was wide eyed and ready, but he tried to look fearless.

"Yo, bro. I want to shake your hand. Anyone who stands up me like this deserves my respect." R.A. offered his monstrous hand, and the two men shook and bumped shoulders like old friends.

R.A. and Borrello became good buddies, and the Bonanno mob enforcer got more jail cred in C-95.

R.A. would eventually get twenty-five to life for homicide,

which was why he was in Rikers to begin with. The sentence for R.A. would be overturned. Gene lost track of his pal. Mitts, on the other hand, got natural life for a double murder two years later.

Louis Romano

BEWARE THE UNSOLVED
MYSTERIES

Whenever Gene Borrello thought he was invincible or acted like his success puffed up his swagger a bit, Uncle Vin Asaro would bring Gene back to normal with a simple thought: "Don't ever think you are bigger than the life."

Asaro's decades of experience in the Mafia made all those around him take his advice as a teaching moment.

Vin Asaro's loyalty to the family usually ended badly for anyone who dared to tread on his people.

Sometime in the early 90s, Ronnie G and his friends went out to Zachary's, a hot-spot in Queens. It was late at night, and people were pretty tanked up. Ronnie G got into an altercation with some older guy. It's not important who was right or what the argument was about. The guy cracked a bottle over Ronnie G's head, shattering the glass everywhere. A piece of the glass cut into Ronnie's throat. One of Ronnie's friends, John Brillo, wrapped his neck in a towel, applying pressure to the wound, and ran Ronnie to the hospital that was across the street from Zachary's. Ronnie had coded twice. He was so near death that a priest gave him last rights.

The doctors at the hospital said the only reason Ronnie had survived was because of John Brillo's quick action.

Borrello picks up the story:

"Uncle Vin Asaro found out who the guy was and did his diligence. The guy who used the bottle on Ronnie was never seen again. He disappeared. Uncle Vin and his son…took care of it.

"Later on, Ronnie would return the favor to John Brillo for saving his life. A Bonanno associate named Jimmy Aurora, aka Jimmy Unit, who was on record as a Bonanno soldier, would get into an altercation with John Brillo, beating him very badly and nearly biting his finger off. After the fight happened, Brillo went to Ronnie G about the situation. Ronnie G lost it and went ballistic. He confronted 'Jackie,' an acting skipper in the Bonanno family, that his man, Jimmy Aurora, beat up a harmless guy that had once saved his life. Ronnie told Jackie he had to be dealt with and that he would handle it with his crew. Jackie explained to Jimmy that he would have to take the beating or else Ronnie was going to kill him. Jackie negotiated for Jimmy to take the beating rather than be clipped.

"Jimmy met up with Ricky Kessler, an enforcer for the Bonanno family and one of Ronnie's best friends from childhood. Ricky began beating the shit out of Jimmy. Standing by in a car were Ronnie G and Mike Palmaccio, also known as Mikey Boats. They jumped out of the car and began beating Jimmy Unit with billy-clubs and slap-jacks, almost crushing his skull in. That was the favor repaid to John Brillo for saving Ronnie G's life.

"One disappeared, one was sent to the hospital, and no one knew anything. Mysteries abound."

THE BUSINESS OF MONEY

In Gene Borrello's own words:

"The most important thing I was to Uncle Vin and Ronnie G was to be their enforcer. If someone didn't pay their gambling debt, or they reneged on a loan, or they were out of line in any way, I was called on. Violence was my stock in trade, and I was very good at it.

"I was taught one thing from the beginning, and very emphatically. Once a person came to us to place bets or to borrow money, they were no longer a civilian. They were then subject to our consequences. Ronnie G's was the central bank of Howard Beach. This was at a time when four major Mafia bosses lived in Howard Beach. Just the vig I would collect for him. Every single day of this would easily total thirty thousand dollars a week. That was just from the money he had on the street. Between Ronnie G's loan sharking and sports book alone, where he was also the bank, it seemed to me that there was no bottom to the availability of cash.

"Oftentimes it is other criminals who need a short-term loan. For example, let's say a guy came to borrow thirty grand. First, they are not approaching Ronnie, no one is speaking to Ronnie, and they are dealing with one of his crew. Once the loan is approved, the 'guy' now pays usually three points, but on a loan the size of thirty thousand, probably would yield two points. That means the guy must pay two percent, or six-hundred dollars per week, vig or vigorish, no matter what. That is just interest. The principal is still thirty thousand and still due and will be due until it's paid in full or until hell freezes over, for you will be paying the devil until you die. And if you borrowed money on a Tuesday, that is your day. Every Tuesday, Gene or 'Genie Boy' would be there to collect. I did all the collections for Ronnie G.

"Ronnie's loan-sharking business was so extensive that he would lend large sums of money to other loan sharks, usually at a rate of one point. They, in turn, would put the money on the street at two or three points, pay Ronnie his one point, and pocket the rest. Ronnie was the central bank of Howard Beach. The business was so extensive that the thirty-thousand-dollar vig per week that I collected would just scratch the surface.

"It's not like a nine-to-five job or a store where you took a salary. I didn't get paid a commission for what I collected for Ronnie G. The way I made money in the loan sharking business, like everyone else in Ronnie's crew, was that he allowed us to lend money. Ronnie provided us with cash that we would all lend out at three points and make two points profit. Personally, I was lending at two points, making only one point profit, but customers were rushing to borrow at a lower rate. In a very short time, I had 250,000 dollars on the street in loans. At one point, I was collecting twenty-five hundred per week profit. This was a nice weekly salary, and all cash. But it was just walking around money. There was more money to be made…much more.

"Then there was the sports book business where Ronnie G was the bank. Sometimes I wondered if there was a bottom to the cash he had available.

"The sports business is no longer a back-room operation filled with phones, a chalk board, and people taking bets. We moved into the twenty-first century. The way Ronnie G set up his sports book would employ using legitimate betting establishments housed in the Caribbean Islands where he would purchase approximately one hundred and fifty betting accounts with an off-shore establishment.

"These accounts were paid for weekly at fifteen dollars per account. To maintain these accounts, Ronnie was paying 2,250 dollars per week. These accounts would be distributed to members of Ronnie's crew based on ability and demand. Ronnie was acting as the bank, and I was handling all the accounts in regards to the distribution to other members of the crew and maintenance of the accounts.

"Having the master password, I could monitor all activity of all the accounts all the time if desired.

"With the sports betting, the guys in the crew, including me, would make money on the half-sheet, and Ronnie would make the remainder. A half-sheet works like this: let's say 'Frankie Bones' Caputo, a top earner in Ronnie's sports book and associate, would get the number of accounts he requests from me, then assign each account to his bettors. The bettors were assigned a code name by me with the betting service. The bettor would enter his bets in his computer; once entered, the bet could not be deleted or changed.

At the end of the week, Sunday night, I would review all the accounts and see who owed what or what we owed. We seldom paid out. Anyway, let's say Frankie Bones's bettors had net losses of thirty grand. Frankie was obligated to collect the money and turn in fifteen grand to me, and he kept fifteen grand, ergo a half sheet, fifty percent for Frankie, and fifty percent for Ronnie G.

"Remember, Ronnie was purchasing one hundred and fifty accounts to cover all the bettors that we brought in. Year-round, on the sports book alone, we were averaging forty grand a week.

"Where the violence came in, and what I enjoyed doing the most, was collecting for Ronnie G if his vig wasn't there on the exact day it was set to be paid. Some weeks, I didn't have to be the enforcer at all.

"For instance, on Super Bowl Sunday in 2013, the Denver Broncos were playing the Seattle Seahawks, and the betting was one-sided, with all of the action going on the Broncos. We took in 150,000 dollars. On my half-sheet, I raked in 25,000 dollars personally. Not a bad day's pay. And everyone paid up, so things were quiet for me.

"Ronnie G arrogantly commented, 'Well, that's the money for the bricks for my new house.' He was just about right. The contract for the bricks on the Giallanzo's massive new home came in at just under 150,000 dollars.

"But there were a few bettors and borrowers who didn't pay up on the due date.

"One time, one of Ronnie G's customers, I'll call him Sal, who owed five hundred dollars a week, to be paid on Fridays, gave me a sob story that he would pay up the following Tuesday. I let him slide but abused him verbally just a little.

45

"I went to Sal's auto repair shop. He looked like he was doing good. All four bays were busy, and customers were waiting in line for their cars to be serviced. The cheap prick even had a vending machine for his customers to buy coffee.

"I looked him straight in the eyes, my black, Nike baseball cap pulled down just above my eyes. I said, 'Business looks really good. You been good for a while with me, Sal. Don't make me look like a fucking asshole to Ronnie. This ain't no joke. It's a business, just like you got here.'

"'No, no. I swear, I just got a little jammed up with some shit with my ex-wife. Tuesday. I'll be here at six in the morning,' Sal stammered.

"'I'll be here at ten. Don't fuck with this, Sally,' I warned.

"Sure enough, when I go there Tuesday, Sal wasn't there. No one knew where he was, and he left no message for me.

"Wednesday morning, I go back. No Sal.

"Thursday, I show up at six in the morning while fuckface Sal is opening the door. I'm already pissed that I had to get up with the birds and that Ronnie is asking me for the vig.

"I come up fast on Sal and smack him hard in the face in front of two of his mechanics. Seeing me and my rage, luckily for them, nobody made a move.

"'What the fuck, Gene?' Sal whimpered

"'What the fuck, Gene? That's what you have to ask me?'

46

I smacked him again.

"'Okay…okay, I got it. Here! Jesus Christ!' Sal dug into his pocket and took out a sizable wad, peeling off the five hundred. He gave me another hundred for my trouble, and I laughed right in his face.

"'Never again, Sally boy. Due on Friday, or I start the day with giving you a nice beating. Understood?'

"This was easy. I'd come into Ronnie G's office in the morning sometimes, and I'd get an assignment. 'Go give so-and-so a beating. Go shoot at so-and-so. Don't hit him, just scare the piss out of him.' Or 'torch his car' or 'shoot this asshole in his legs.' I did it with a smile on my face. I loved it."

Gene Borrello talked about treachery every time I interviewed him. Treachery was a word that everyone in the life was forced to live with on a daily basis. Sometimes it was obvious that a member was being betrayed and set up, and then there were times where the deceitfulness was more subtle. However, there were times that Gene Borrello and his friends and his crew members got themselves in trouble for being treacherous and deceitful themselves.

Gene Borrello told me the story of the perfect example of the danger their nefarious actions put them in. This time, their own treachery almost cost two of Borrello's closest friends their lives.

In 2005, Borrello's good friend, Ronnie Manns, got out of jail after doing a five-to-fifteen-year bid for armed robbery and attempted murder. Manns did ten years on the sentence. In an upstate New York Prison, Manns was called "The Thing" because of his huge size. He was so big that he looked distorted.

Manns came up with a plan to rob some kilos of cocaine off of a Queens Dominican drug dealing crew who were notorious for violence. Like everything else in the life, the rush was in the stealing and the getting away with it. The fact that these Dominicans were tied to a Mexican cartel with, in Borrello's own words, "infinity money" was just a detail worth the risk to Ronnie Manns. These ruthless drug dealers would slaughter the children of their enemies just to send a message.

Manns found out about the potential score and didn't have to share the proceeds with anyone. Manns joined with Mike Palmaccio, a made guy in Jerry Asaro's crew. Manns would go on record with Palmaccio a few years later, but for now, Manns wasn't sharing with anyone in the Bonanno Family that wasn't going to be doing the heavy lifting. Manns had some catching up to do after being inside for a decade. So much for jail time reforming a criminal mind.

Scoring two kilos of high-quality coke off the Dominicans in those days netted Manns 50,000 dollars cash.

Less than a month after the heist, on a clear, crisp, Thanksgiving night, right on Cross Bay Boulevard in Ozone Park, Queens, across from Aldo's Pizzeria, Manns was sitting in his black Mercedes Benz 550 with his friend Teddy, a knockaround guy.

Standing on the street was a gorgeous, mid-twenties

Latina wearing a short, black leather jacket with four-inch high heels, exposing her luscious ass through a pair of black, skin-tight jeans.

Ronnie Manns lowered his tinted window to engage the girl in conversation. At first, she played hard to get, but Manns persisted, throwing not-so-subtle pick-up lines at her. Finally, the sexy girl smiled and started walking over to the Benz. Manns was thrilled that his lines worked.

As she came closer to the open window, the hot Latina took out a nine-millimeter pistol that she had stashed on her back under the leather jacket. She pointed the gun at Manns's head. Manns grabbed the gun just as she began firing. Several shots went into Teddy's side before Manns was able to wrestle the gun away.

The smoking-hot girl fled to a waiting vehicle, and she was gone in an instant down Cross Bay Boulevard. The hit on Ronnie Manns was a bust, and Teddy would survive his wounds.

The girl was brought up for the day from the Dominican Republic for a paltry 2500 dollars to kill Manns and take retribution for the stolen kilos. She would be on the next flight to the DR, and Manns would have to wait for the next time the Dominicans would try to effect their revenge. Looking over your shoulder was a way of life in the life.

PINCHED

In the street, Gene Borrello wore casual clothing. When he went to collect money for Ronnie G or Uncle Vin Asaro, he would show up wearing a t-shirt, shorts, jogging pants, or black chinos, and sneakers. Unlike the older guard in the well-known Gambino family who emulated their boss, John Gotti, with flashy and tapered leisure suits, Borrello looked as if he was making a delivery for a pizzeria.

On this particularly memorable day that signaled a major change in his life, Borrello recalled the events:

"You would have thought I'd have felt out of place walking down the street in a tuxedo, but my mind was preoccupied, and I didn't care in the slightest.

"My mind was always racing -there was constantly something to do, something to contemplate. I played life like a game of chess, always looking for my next move. Living and breathing a life of crime, there was always the next move and the moves after that.

"Murder was on my mind more and more frequently. I knew it would be just a matter of time before someone was going to die."

With Samantha, his girlfriend at the time, Borrello flew in from Florida just after midnight to attend a wedding. Sam was a short, blonde, Italian knockout with a smoking body. Borrello was as close to being in love that he thought was ever possible. He was too intent on making a name for himself and winning the prize of becoming a made man.

GENE BORRELLO
Mafia Enforcer for the Bonanno Crime Family

Borrello continued his story:

"I was a groomsman in Mike Pecchio's wedding. Mike and I were childhood friends, the kind of friendship that would last a lifetime, no matter what. When the plane landed, my cousin picked us up at John F. Kennedy airport. We would be staying in Centerville, Queens, with my other cousin, Frank, who had a three-bedroom apartment that was close to the church."

Gene and Sam were dropped at Frank's apartment. They talked with Frank and his gal, Courtney, to catch up on the gossip of Howard Beach for a half-hour and then headed to bed.

The morning came quickly. Borrello was up at nine o'clock, showered, dressed, and out the door. He planned to meet Samantha at the church. He walked to another friend's house, and from there, he was picked up to meet with the bridal party to take pictures.

"While walking along the street, my mind wandered for just a moment. I had walked only a block, and all hell broke loose.

Loud shouting coming from all directions, 'Stop! Don't move!' And a lot of cursing and screaming. I never got to the wedding," Gene recalled.

There were twelve to fifteen detectives and plain-clothes cops converging on Borrello, guns drawn. He was quickly handcuffed, placed in the backseat of an unmarked police car, and whisked away to the local precinct. Detective Jerry McNeely pulled no punches. "I'm gonna make sure you get a 500,000-dollar bail while you rot on Rikers

Island." Borrello's charges were enough to put him in prison for many years. In New York State, Genie Boy was indicted for Possession of a Firearm, Selling Guns, and Conspiracy to Commit Home Invasion. In the State of Florida, the charge was Conspiracy to Commit a Robbery in the First Degree. The federal indictments were Conspiracy to Commit Murder, Attempted Murder, Home Invasion, and RICO Assault.

SUMMER OF 2006

The summer of 2006 saw a lot of chaos and treachery. Gene Borrello was in his prime, and his violence hit the high mark. Borrello was the first to admit how severe he had become under Vinnie Asaro and Ronnie G as he worked his way to be straightened out.

He dreamed of being a made man, to the point that he was willing to do anything to achieve his goal.

"Being around Ronnie G, working for him, there was always the possibility of blood being spilled. The problem, whether you realize it or not, I was like a gun with a hair trigger. Sometimes you react or overreact for no reason at all. On one occasion, Chris Cognata and I walked into a small, neighborhood grocery store.

Chris had spied a guy named Phil Gallina. The guy wasn't well liked by anyone in our neighborhood. He was obnoxious, spoiled, and a wannabe gangster. In reality, he was a spoiled, rich kid from Howard Beach who wanted to dabble in gangster life but did not have the balls for the life. He was one of many.

"Chris and I picked up a couple of items for a snack. While leaving the store, Chris and Phil momentarily locked eyes. Chris being Chris, he automatically said, 'What the fuck you lookin' at?' Phil tried to act tough, but before he could do anything, Chris broke a full bottle of Snapple over the guy's head. We hit him a few times and left him sprawled on the floor. For us and the life we led, this event was no outlier. It was just another day. But this incident would cause an incredible chain of events to occur later on."

Chris Cognata was tough. With lightning-fast hands, he hit like a hammer. His thick neck made it harder to be knocked out in a fight, and he had a nasty temperament. This was a guy who basically did what he wanted with no regard for anyone or, for that matter, himself, because he never considered the consequences.

Borrello goes on, recollecting the events with crystal clear recall:

"Both of us were from Howard Beach. We would become good friends, and our paths would cross many times, not always good.

"When Chris was seventeen, he had words with an older guy, Ronnie Salerno, who was twenty-five. It got to the point where they were going to fight. Both guys knew each other, were from the same neighborhood, and good sense prevailed so they didn't fight. But after they walked away, Ronnie Salerno was still upset. Salerno was an up-and-coming gangster and was being looked at by Ronnie

G. Well Salerno, upset over the entire incident, was talking trash, saying how he would have beat Cognata's ass, and stated that the next time he saw him, he was going to fuck him up. Salerno's comments got back to Chris, who in turn went to Ronnie G and Mike Palmaccio to ask to fight Salerno. They said okay and set up a fight between Ronnie Salerno and Chris Cognata in three days.

"The fight was an upset, to say the least. Chris Cognata beat the piss out of Ronnie Salerno. He had two black eyes, and I don't think Salerno landed a punch. That fight ended any chance Salerno had at being around Ronnie G. As a matter of fact, right after the fight, Ronnie G said to Palmaccio, 'He's with you,' meaning Salerno was not good enough to be around Ronnie G. Today, Ronnie Salerno has a job as a civil servant driving a school bus."

Driving a school bus and getting out of the life was likely the best thing that ever happened to Salerno and his family. As so many in the life will agree, the life had a lousy retirement plan.

Borrello continues his eyewitness reporting:

"Even at the age of twenty-one, living the lifestyle I was living, hanging around with guys like Chris Cognata...it had brought about some surprises. On one occasion, Chris and I and some guys from the neighborhood went to a club for a night out. While we were there, Phil Gallina pops in. Chris broke his balls a bit, but no one thought anything of it. Nothing special, no problems, just a night out on the town. One of the guys who had driven had left early, leaving one car for the rest of us when we would finally leave. Six of us would have to pile into an Audi A8. Four guys in the backseat and two in the front. DiGangi was driving. Chris Cognata was in the front passenger seat. Me, Burga, Billy Dublin, Frankie Roccaforte, and Danny Crocker were jammed in the back seat.

"We took off, got onto Grand Central Parkway, were cruising along, virtually no traffic at all, music blasting in the car, windows down, air coursing through the car. We were all enjoying ourselves. No one was paying attention to anything other than what was going on in the car. I remember looking to my left and seeing a black Mercedes Benz CLK with flames coming from the front passenger window. I turned to Burger and asked, 'Did we just get shot at?' Burger said, 'Yeah.' We heard a gurgling sound coming from Crocker.

"Somebody yelling said, 'Crocker got hit.' DiGangi pulled the car over, and we got Crocker out of the car and laid him on the side of the road. Crocker was shot through the neck, bleeding profusely. Burger had the presence of mind to wrap Crocker's neck with a shirt and apply pressure until help arrived. Once Crocker was more or less stable, we also learned Billy Dublin had been grazed along his back. One of the guys called 911. The ambulance arrived on the scene first, and they immediately took Dublin and Crocker, rushing them to the hospital. I would learn later if it was not for Burger wrapping Crocker's neck and maintaining constant pressure, Crocker would have certainly died. Burger saved his life.

"Next on the scene were the cops, the blue-and-white cars and the plain Chevy Impalas the detectives drive. The detectives were running the scene, instructing the officers what to do. They immediately took me and Billy Dublin in separate cars to their precinct. The detectives took each of us to separate interrogation rooms. The detectives' first and only question was, 'Who did it?' They believed we had to know and maintained the pressure. So much so that while questioning me, one of the detectives said, 'Well, your friend just died.' They were grasping at straws. Evidently, they knew me and Billy were in the life and had hoped that by telling us Crocker had died, we would be overcome with grief and anger, giving up the shooter. Nope. Our only intention was to kill the shooter.

"The detectives would keep me and Dublin at the precinct

for ten hours in the interrogation rooms.

"For me, this routine was banal. By this time, I was twenty-one, a criminal, had done time, been through multiple interrogations. I had no intention of telling these guys anything. The detectives let Dublin go a bit sooner than me, but not by much. You have to understand something...when you're in the criminal life, even as the victim, or in a situation like this, you're still a suspect.

"Once the detective released me, I called my mother, and she came and picked me up outside the precinct. I opened the car door to my mother's car, no sleep for over twenty-four hours, still fueled by adrenaline. I got in and asked, 'Is he dead?' My mother responded, 'No, but it's not looking good.' We headed to the hospital to see how Crocker was doing. We walked in and saw a lot of people. The mood was somber from our neighborhood.

"Crocker was in surgery with a serious gunshot wound. No one would say the words, but we all thought Crocker was dead. We were waiting for a doctor to tell us he was gone.

"While I was mulling about in the waiting-room, I managed to recover some semblance of normal thought, and I saw Burger and flashed back to the sight of his blood-soaked shirt when he was helping Crocker.

"I don't remember much more, except when I finally went to see Crocker after his successful surgery. We would learn that he had died twice during the surgery.

"Being in his room, with him in recovery, the sight of Crocker's neck was unbelievable -it had swelled to an incredible size from the gunshot he sustained.

"Crocker was not a Mafia wannabe. He was a regular, hard-working guy trying make his way in life. Crocker was simply a regular, blue-collar guy who went out for a night on the town that turned out to be nearly his last. Later, we found out he was shot with a nine-millimeter bullet, and when the car was recovered, the detectives had found that eight rounds were fired into the car.

"From the moment we were shot at, I realized who this was coming from. It was no coincidence we were shot at after leaving Club Remi, the same night Phil Gallina was at the club. We knew Phil had something to do with Crocker being shot. I approached people who were friendly to Phil and began to pressure them. I would discover Phil had left for Italy. Actually, he left the day after the shooting. He obviously had a plan. Phil leaving for Italy was all the proof we needed. He did it, two and two make four; this was not a courtroom where there is guilt beyond a reasonable doubt, this was the street. My plan to get Phil to return was simple. I took a Tec-Nine nine-millimeter and fired seventeen rounds into his family's house with everyone home. Two weeks later, I set Phil's sister's car ablaze. I would force this guy to return to face what he did. But he would not comply. Two weeks after that, I shot the house up again. After approximately a month, Phil would return to the United States. It was made clear to Phil's cousin, nothing and no one was going to stop until Phil was dead. Phil was in the area, but laying low. A couple of months later, I would find out from one of the head Albanians that Phil knew of a couple of Albanian guys who would be paid ten thousand dollars to do the shooting. In reality, it was a botched hit. If I couldn't kill Gallina, I would do anything I could to him. After everything that happened, the family realized it would not end. The house would be vacated, put up for sale, and they would move away from the neighborhood. The family would move to Middle Village, Queens.

"This entire ordeal had started because Chris Cognata had beaten up Phil Gallina, and I had helped him. By some act of God, us hunting Phil would come to an end because of Chris Cognata."

QUEENS

There was no shortage of bad guys in Queens. One after another, new names and faces poped up while Borrello, with perfect recall, named the people that he spent his time with on a daily basis. The stories never ceased to amaze the listener.

"Nick 'Pudgie' Festa was an associate with Ronnie G at that time. Before he became an associate, he was a drug dealer. When he got around Ronnie G, by La Cosa Nostra rule, his drug dealing had to stop. Pudgie would take a step or two back, put in a front man or two to be the face of the business.

"The money would keep rolling in, and his cash hoard would continue to grow. With the excessive cash flow, Pudgie would reinvest in the shylock business, putting his cash on the street. Pudgie was Ronnie G's biggest earner at that time, bringing Ronnie eight to ten grand a week. Pudgie was known amongst Ronnie's crew as the Golden Goose. Everything the guy touched turned to gold.

"But Pudgie had one fault, and it was simple and evident: he was weak. The guy was not prone to violence, it simply wasn't his way. In the life, when you are making big money, you need to be feared or you become prey for the hungry. After seven home invasions, Pudgie realized he had two choices: retire or gravitate towards the mob. Ronnie G took him in with open arms.

Gene Borrello had box seats to witness the Pudgie -Ronnie G relationship.

"Now with Ronnie G, anyone taking Pudgie's money was guilty of taking Ronnie G's money. They'd take on the full weight of Ronnie and his crew, who were willing to do whatever Ronnie G ordered, including murder, for there would have to be consequences. But there is always that one guy that does not care. This time, it was Chris Cognata. .

"During the winter of 2005 or 2006, Pudgie would be robbed again. When he exited his car, two armed guys wearing ski masks converged on him. Sticking a gun in his ribs, they escorted Pudgie into his house, where his wife and child were also.

"The armed robbers put the son in the bathroom and secured Pudgie and his wife using zipties. Pudgie gave up the valuables he had in the house. They made off with approximately one hundred and fifty thousand in cash and sixty thousand in jewelry.

"This shed some light on the home invaders. Pudgie would tell Ronnie that one of the guys patted his wife on the ass. Ronnie G was a devout family man.

"The fact that Pudgie's wife and kid were home was bad enough, but hearing that one of the guys patted Pudgie's wife on her ass put him over the edge.

"Ronnie G and I, guys involved in crime, know what other criminals are doing, that's our business. We know who's dealing drugs, running a book, who are bank robbers, armored car guys, burglars, boosters, car thieves, and so on, and naturally, home invaders, too. Remember, Pudgie's home invasion was not random, it was someone who knew he was making big money, had the balls to do it, and had no fear of the mob. Me, Ronnie, Padavona, and the rest of the crew were throwing out names, possible candidates to be investigated. Sooner or later, we would get to the bottom of it. The criminal circle is small, and it would be just a matter of time before we would have some concrete evidence.

"By sheer luck, someone would be pulled over, a gun found in the car, along with a cache of jewelry. The guy was arrested and the evidence impounded by the cops. Word in the neighborhood had spread; the following day, we found out that Chris Cognata and Mike Izzo were the guys that got arrested the previous night. A few days later, Ronnie G would confirm that Chris did the piece of work. Some of Cognata's guys were even bragging about the job in the neighborhood.

"Pudgie was an associate of Ronnie G's. He was robbed. He was making Ronnie money. One of the robbers smacked Pudgie's wife on the ass, and lastly, bragged about the home invasion in the neighborhood, rubbing Ronnie's face in it. They went too far. There would have to be retribution.

"Chris realized his boasting about the robbery had gotten back to Ronnie G, and I assume he panicked.

"Ronnie called all of us to his house to let us know Chris had been there, swearing he had nothing to do with Pudgie being robbed. And he persuaded Ronnie, saying it's people from the neighborhood spreading false information because Chris terrorized the neighborhood.

"Chris's argument was true. Ronnie gave Chris the benefit of the doubt, but an investigation would continue.

"Please understand, while Mafia life is violent, when matters like this arise, there is a thorough investigation before action is taken. Criminals, unlike government agents, are not bound by rules, the Constitution, ethics, or morals. You get caught lying, you may get a beating.

"Chris convinced Ronnie, or at least raised enough doubt that it may not have been him. The investigation would continue. The crew searched high and low, but in our hearts, we knew it was Chris; we were trying to find more information to confirm our beliefs. Somehow, unbeknownst to me, Ronnie would obtain information that conclusively proved Chris was one of the home invaders.

"A short time later, we would learn Ronnie Manns was the second guy.

"Ronnie G was mad that Chris had the nerve to come to his house, plead innocence, and lie to his face.

"Ronnie gave me and Bobby G the job: send him a message-shoot him, but don't kill him.

"Bobby G and I were actively hunting Chris Cognata, but we weren't having any luck. One of the guys in Ronny G's crew, Ricky Kessler, was close with Chris. Ronnie G would have Ricky call Chris, have him come to meet Ricky at a remote location to set a trap. Ronnie had Ricky call with all of us there and with the phone on speaker because Ronnie G wanted to hear. Ricky told Chris to meet him at Gold's gym. Chris said he'd be there. The area where

Gold's gym was located provided several hides, and late at night, midnight, it was not well lit, the perfect spot. But Chris never showed. He was either wise beyond his years or had been tipped off. We would continue to look for Chris. Finding him was a priority.

The passage of time would not lessen the offense.

"A month passed before Chris found me at Lindenwood, Howard Beach. In reality, I found him at a four-way stop.

"I happened to be there because Vinny Mineo had called me, told me to meet him at the intersection that was a block from my apartment, so I walked to meet him. Vinny and I concluded our business, made small talk, and I started heading back to my apartment. While walking down the street, I see a green Acura TL twodoor coming at me. Chris's girl was driving. Chris was in the front passenger seat. He was genuinely surprised to see me. The car came to a stop, and Chris got out, his arms in the air spread wide, saying, 'Are you lookin' for me?' I answered, 'what are you talkin' about?' I needed to lure him closer to me to put a bullet or two in him. Chris was coming around the car to talk, as soon as he got in front of the car, I drew a Beretta .380 from my waist, cycled a round into the chamber, raised the gun to fire. Chris's eyes widened when he saw my actions and began to run. I squeezed off four rounds. Chris's girlfriend reacted instinctively, running the car into me, stopping the shooting midstream. I discovered later Chris had been hit in his forearm."

Having just shot a guy in his own neighborhood, on a busy street in his own neighborhood, Chris knew he had to get out of the area. Gene Borrello had used his thirty-eight

Smith and Wesson handgun to shoot Chris Cognata. Borrello knew Chris had to leave. He immediately called Mike Padavona, who showed up minutes later.

"I got him," Borrello blurted inside Padavona's car. Gene realized he had a bad pain in the heel of his right foot. He was scraped up badly from being hit by the car, and his right heel was smashed up pretty good.

Padavona smartly called their friend, Burger. Gene would hide out in his apartment for the night.

The next day, Gene went to see Ronnie G, who was pleased by Gene's retribution.

Gene announced, "We just shot a pit bull. He's gonna retaliate big-time."

In real wiseguy fashion, Ronnie G replied, "He ain't doing nothin'. Fuck him."

Gene continued, "Chris is just pissed off that I caught him by surprise. I heard he's telling everyone he fell off a four-wheeler, and that's why his arm is bandaged up. He'll never admit I shot him in the arm."

"He got my message loud and clear. You steal my money and rob one of my guys, and you get shot," Ronnie G added.

About a month later, Cognata sent Ronnie a message. There was Frankie "Fucks" Ran, a guy they used as a gofer to go upstate to purchase bullets, mow the lawn, and whatever else Ronnie or one of the guys in the crew needed. The crew took care of the guy, who was unemployed. Frankie "Fucks" picked up some needed cash doing errands, odd jobs, and being discrete.

Frankie was out with his girl one day,. He went into a candy store, and Chris Cognata happened in right behind him. Frankie, while a gofer, was still part of Ronnie's crew. Chris, without warning, started in on Frankie, beating him up badly. When Chris finished beating Frankie, he told him, "I see any of Ronnie's crew, I'm gettin' yas."

Ronnie G was made aware of Frankie's beating. He didn't take the news well. It became a declaration of war.

Ronnie told his crew that if anyone was seen, known, or friendly with Chris, they were targets for a severe beating.

Borrello moved quickly, "We took what Ronnie said and put it on the street to forewarn everyone around Chris and the neighborhood. The first victim was Phil Cannon. We knew he was still seeing Chris; we would go to his house. Ronnie G, Ricky Kessler, and I went to the house. We had Ricky go to the door. Had it been me or Ronnie, he would not have answered. Phil opened the door and Kessler, without warning, hit him on his nose. Kessler, at six-foot-three, two hundred and twenty points, and an athlete, was formidable. His one punch did damage. Phil was out, nose broken, blood all over the floor. Me and Ronnie emerged from our hide to enter the house. We saw Phil laid out, and Phil's dog started barking.

"Ronnie G, the big gangster, is deathly afraid of dogs, and took off running back to the truck. I was right behind him. Come to find out it was some tiny mutt. Kessler, while we ran to the truck, nonchalantly walked to the truck and got in.

That's the one thing I liked, actually we all liked, about Ronnie G. He doesn't just give orders, he is right there with you. This quality made us very loyal to him.

"These beatings were not random, not by a long shot. Ronnie G's crew had eyes all over Howard Beach, and people were eager to pass on any information to remain in or get into the good graces of Ronnie G.

"Naturally, we wanted Chris Cognata, but he was living outside of Howard Beach, changing cars frequently, and sneaking in and out of the area. He was a crafty, elusive adversary. We targeted anyone supporting or aiding him in any way.

About one week after the Phil Cannon incident, we received information that John Michael was seen with Chris Cognata. Frankie "Bones" Caputo, one of Ronnie's crew, knew John.

Ronnie G orchestrated the plan. He had Bones go to John's house, call him on his cell from just outside, and lure him out. When John came out, Bones waved to him, calling him over. John approached, and when close enough, Bones punched him, knocking John to the ground. Me and Bobby G had been waiting just around the corner, ran over, and began beating John with a fish beater and a baseball bat. He managed to get up, fleeing for his life, He made it to his house. We followed him in, continuing to beat the guy. One of John's parents began screaming, 'I'm calling the cops.' We fled, got in the car where Ronnie G was waiting for us, and we sped off. Bones left in his own vehicle. We wanted it known to one and all, if we couldn't get to Chris, we wanted him isolated."

Like the branches on a tree, one by one, Borrello and the other members of Ronnie G's crew were cutting ties with Cognata and his world. It would be just a matter of time before Chris Cognata would be by himself.

Borrello stated, "Overzealousness was high amongst all of us. Frankie "Fucks" called Mike Padavona and told him, 'I'm being chased by Chris in a white Lexus Jeep.'

"Frankie was now deathly afraid of Cognata from the severe beating Chris had given him. Padavona told Frankie, 'Lure him to the boathouse.'

Padavona owned a boathouse on Crossbay Boulevard behind a Honda dealership that sold recreational equipment: motorcycles, four wheelers, and the like. The dealership, owned by Padavona's brother-in-law and his family, owned all the docks in that area. The boathouse was the primary hangout of the crew. Padavona had set it up with a card table, television, refrigerator, coffee maker, chairs, couch, and it was right on the water. This spot, for the time being, was command central for Ronnie G's crew.

"We would plot, plan, and scheme at the boathouse. And now, Frankie 'Fucks' was going to drop Chris Cognata right into our laps. 'Fucks' was bringing Chris right to us."

Ronnie G, Bobby G, Ricky Kessler, and Palmaccio were all there. Borrello was armed with a Hi-Point .380 pistol (Saturday night special).

Borrello continued the story:

"We all went outside. I asked Ronnie G, 'What should I do?' Ronnie said, 'Shoot into the car.' I could see the white Lexus RX330 Jeep coming right toward us, making a left on Crossbay Boulevard and driving into my line of fire. I started shooting with my pistol.

"Shooting into the front of the Jeep and continuing as the car made the turn onto the Boulevard, I emptied the gun, firing six rounds into the Jeep.

"As the saying goes, 'If it sounds too good to be true, it usually is.' About ten minutes later, I get a call on my cell from Joey 'Goggles' Astremo; he was a drug dealer Bobby G and I were shaking down.

"Terrified, Goggles said, 'Why you shootin' at us?' I asked him, 'Why you with Chris?' Goggles replied, 'Chris ain't even in the car.' The car was owned by Allison Brown, a girl Chris had been dating. The bullets that struck the car had rendered it inoperable. They were still in the area, but pulled over. After

the shooting I had gotten in, Fucks took me in his car out of the immediate area. Shortly thereafter, I received a call to go to Padavona's house. Frankie 'Fucks' drove us there. We got out of the car. Ronnie G was furious, hollering at Frankie, 'You said Chris was in the car.' Frankie said, 'I think so,' stuttering and scared, for Ronnie was seeing red. Ronnie slapped Frankie hard, hollering, 'Whatta you think this is, a fucking game?' There had been three people in the Lexus Jeep, thank God no one got shot, for these people were civilians. Two days later, I would find out one of the stray bullets from the shooting would penetrate the door of another car and just missed the woman driving.

"While Chris Cognata may not have been in the car,

the shooting scared the life out of the girl he was dating. After that, Allison Brown was done with Chris; there was another person we alienated. Ronnie G, though he was upset, actually liked what happened.

"Another person who had been told to stay away from Chris Cognata by Borrello was Mike 'Cuzzo' Izzo. Chris and Cuzzo were friends. Cuzzo was supplying Chris with weapons to protect himself and drugs to help him make money. Cuzzo did not heed the crew's warning to stay away from Chris.

"Ronnie Manns, a friend to Chris, had been playing both sides. Ronnie was the double agent and a solid source of information. Bobby G and I met with Ronnie Manns to see if he had any information on Cuzzo. He didn't hesitate. He immediately said, 'Yeah, I know where one of his grow houses is.'"

Borrello goes on, "Bobby and I brought the information to Ronnie G. Without hesitation, Ronnie said to go rob the place. Five of us headed to Atlantic Avenue in Queens. Bones and Pudgie were in one car, armed, keeping watch, while we went to burgle the building. Ricky Kessler, Bobby G, and I went for the second-floor apartment. Ricky, with a crowbar in hand, was working the door when the owner of the apartment came upon us and asked, 'What are yas doin'?' I answered, 'We're friends of Mike.' The woman, in her mid-thirties, knew the contents of the apartment. She also knew we were there to rob Cuzzo. Instead of calling the police, she called Cuzzo. We made our way into the apartment. The apartment was huge -three bedrooms and nothing but pot throughout, growing from floor to ceiling. There was the equipment to maintain the plants and a television. We tore the plants down and began stuffing them into trash bags. What we couldn't take, we destroyed. All the lamps, the climate control equipment, everything was destroyed, and there was thousands of dollars of damage done to Cuzzo's operation. As we were exiting the apartment, Cuzzo pulled up in his car. We ignored him, threw some of the bags of pot into Pudgie's car, and I got in with Pudgie and Bones. Kessler and Bobby G got in their car, and we took off in different directions.

"Cuzzo chose to follow us, big mistake. Ours was the car with guns inside; we were leading Cuzzo back to Howard Beach. He was persistent, he knew we were entering our neighborhood, and he would not relent. We lured him to a remote block and opened up. Bones, in the backseat, leaned out of the window, and I leaned out of the passenger's seat, and we began to shoot into Cuzzo's vehicle. I fired three or four times with the .38 Special, and Bones fired several rounds from a .380 automatic.

Cuzzo's car swerved to avoid the barrage of bullets, and he sped off in a different direction.

"We met up later at Padavona's, took a look at the weed, but it was no good, still too wet. We just wanted to salvage some money for our trouble. Ronnie G was also there with Padavona. We explained everything that had happened. All this action concluded about one o'clock in the morning; once we reported in, everybody went home. Bobby G and I drove Ricky Kessler home. Two minutes after we dropped off Ricky, I got a call. Four guys were parked at Ricky's house, and one of them was Cuzzo. Words were exchanged, and they open fired on Kessler as he was entering his house. Kessler went diving into his entryway. Once we received Kessler's SOS call, being still in the car, we quickly turned around and raced to Kessler's. While in transit, I called Padavona and Ronnie G, and we got to Kessler's within minutes. Mike and Ronnie arrived about ten minutes later. We made sure Kessler was all right to stay in his house for the night and made sure his wife and two kids were unharmed. The kids were six and seven at the time, and they were cute. They would tease me, calling me stupid Gene in their little mocking voices. We broke for the night, nobody staying with Kessler. We would meet the next day at the boathouse to figure out our next step or attack.

"Ronnie G wanted to know, how did Cuzzo know to return to the grow house? I told him it was the Indian broad, the landlord, that instead of calling the cops, she called Cuzzo. She would be next. Ronnie G instantly said, 'Go shoot the house up, make sure they're home.' Kessler, Bobby G, and I loaded up, just pistols, went to the woman's apartment, and started shooting. Kessler was driving, Bobby G and I had our arms extended out the windows of the passenger's side of the car. We fired about sixteen rounds into the house with no regard for the owner. Once she knowingly provided permission for a grow house and called Cuzzo to tip him off, she was no longer a civilian, she was in our world."

The next day, Borrello received a call from Ronnie Manns, who was calling to setup a "sit-down" with Ronnie G. Manns was comfortable calling Borrello because they were friendly and did some business together. Manns would provide ounces of coke, guns, basically anything that Genie Boy needed. He was one of those guys that if he didn't have what someone wanted, he had a source. Manns was calling on behalf of Cuzzo.

Cuzzo was waving a white flag; he wanted to straighten things out because they truly were getting out of control.

"'I told you, Manns, I'll call you right back. Let me go see Ronnie.' Bobby G and I were together when I got the call. Since this problem started with Cognata, we were together every day. We went to see Ronnie G, and I explained the call from Manns on Cuzzo's behalf. Told Ronnie Cuzzo was asking for a sit-down.

Ronnie G, without hesitation, had me call Manns back and tell him we'll meet right now at Starbucks. When I called, Manns answered the phone and told me to, 'hold on,' and gave the phone to Cuzzo.

"'Right now, at Starbucks.' Cuzzo was concerned about being shot and asked for assurances. I told him, 'I'm with him now, no one's going to hurt you.'

"The meeting went off without any problems. Cuzzo pleaded his case to Ronnie G, telling him, I know Gene since he was a kid, I did not shoot at Kessler, and it was Chris Cognata. Ronnie G accepted what Cuzzo was saying as the truth, but emphasized to Cuzzo that he would hold him responsible. Ronnie G explained to Cuzzo that if he saw him with Cognata, he would be done; his business around here would be ruined. Cuzzo accepted what Ronnie said, knowing the weight of Ronnie G's words and his authority in the criminal world. The meeting they had just outside of Starbucks had concluded after fifteen minutes. Ronnie Manns was waiting at a respectful distance while they talked. As soon as they shook hands and parted company, Manns approached, calling for

Ronnie G. Manns had reiterated what Cuzzo had said about Cognata shooting at Kessler and stressed it was not his brother who shot at Kessler. Manns also had provided Ronnie G with an address of where Chris Cognata was hiding. Ronnie thanked him. Manns let him know he was really good friends with his nephew, Bobby G, and Gene. Manns knew I was Ronnie G's go-to guy and knew one day, I would be a made member. For Manns to help the way he did showed loyalty to Ronnie G, and now he had a chip in the game. It was smart, too, on Manns's part, for things were further escalating and getting out of control.

"After their meeting, we all got together at the boathouse, where Ronnie G explained what occurred with his 'sit-down' with Manns and Cuzzo. Our action was working; Cognata was now alienated from Manns and Cuzzo. Cuzzo had been a key resource to Cognata; not having him to turn to would make hiding out that much more difficult. But more importantly, Ronnie G had walked away with a vital piece of information, a strong prospect of Cognata's location.

"The address and Cognata's presence would have to be verified. The next day, Bobby G and I headed out to the area. We parked far enough away where we would not be noticed. After a short while, we sat in the backseat to survey the entrance without raising suspicions. Luck would have it that there was only one point of entry. We had previously learned that Cognata resorted to moving around the city in the early morning hours: three, four in the morning. And he had been staying with various family members: aunts, uncles, and his grandmother. The address we were watching was his grandmother's -we had recognized her car. Finally, this would be over. After a cumulative period of eight to twelve hours, our stakeout surveillance yielded no results. Though we did not verify Cognata's presence there, we believed Ronnie Manns was telling the truth. It was, in fact, the guy's grandmother's house, and he probably was inside.

"The next day, Ronnie G would raise the stakes. Sometime in the morning, Ronnie G instructed Bobby G and Gene to lay on him. Bobby G had something pressing to do, so he couldn't make it. Ronnie G had a backup plan. 'Don't worry about it, I was sending Palmaccio anyway,' he instructed Gene. The plan was for Palmaccio and Gene to watch the house. They were both armed, and when they saw Cognata, they were to open fire on him. Not to kill him, but to hurt him. How an order like that can be successful is highly questionable. The problem in itself had not escalated to Cognata being murdered, but Ronnie G wanted him shot."

Gene Borrello continues the story:

"Four of us headed out the following night after the surveillance. Padavona was driving, Ronnie G was in the passenger seat. They dropped me and Palmaccio off, and we stayed just across the street from Cognata's hideout. The area provided natural cover, allowing us to easily conceal ourselves. While kneeling behind bushes and other various locations in the immediate area, a couple of hours had passed. Someone finally emerged; I nudged Palmaccio, telling him in an excited whisper, 'The door's opening, get ready, get ready!'When I looked at Palmaccio, I noticed the hand holding the gun was shaking; looking at his face, his nervousness was apparent. Luckily for Palmaccio, the guy coming out of the house was not Cognata. Another two hours would pass, no activity, no one coming in or out. My cell vibrated; it was Ronnie G. He said, 'Come on back, he's not here.' Palmaccio and I got up and walked down the street to where Ronnie and Padavona were parked. Everybody was spent; Ronnie G started the car and pulled away. He drove back to the boat house, giving all of us off the next day. We got in our cars and went our separate ways.

"This was the first free day we had in the past two months or more. We were literally hunting Cognata every single day. Having the next day off, I would go to a club with Palmaccio to have some fun. Try to relax."

The hot spot was Club Posh, a high-end club in Garden City, Long Island. Professional athletes and other celebrities had been known to frequent the spot.

After a while, Palmaccio was wrecked, too drunk to drive. Gene insisted on driving until the disagreeable Palmaccio relented. On the way back, Palmaccio wanted to stop at a neighborhood bar named Glenpatricks. Palmaccio loved this spot; when he walked in the door, he was the celebrated made guy, the local Mafioso. Palmaccio would play the role of the gangster while at Glenpatricks. At other spots, he was in the shadow of Ronnie G, but here, he was the guy. A big fish in a small pond.

Gene picks up the story, "For all of Palmaccio's shortcoming's, in a nutshell, he didn't garner the fear or respect commensurate with being a made member in a major Mafia crime family, but he would fight at the drop of a hat. Mike, being six foot, two inches tall and two hundred and twenty pounds, made him formidable. Supposedly with a night off, when we entered Glenpatricks, work dropped in our laps. The question was whether or not Palmaccio want to press the issue, because I was fine taking no action. When Palmaccio and I walked into Glenpatricks, we spied a guy named Mike Ferena, who was a friend of Chris Cognata's. He was also a close friend of mine. Palmaccio instantly said, 'There's Mike, he's the one hangin' out with Chris.' I told Palmaccio, 'We're off tonight,' hoping he would leave it alone.

Palmaccio said, 'No we're not.' Ferena was sitting at the bar, oblivious to the position he was in; he was happy to see me, saying, 'What's up, Gene?' With that, Palmaccio punched him in the face. Ferena recovered quickly from the punch and, made it out the side door and started running. Palmaccio and I ran after him, but we were winded immediately. Out of the blue, like the Flash, a guy called 'Frankie the Kid' blew by us in full stride. Ferena had a forty-yard head start. Frankie was running like an Olympic sprinter; he closed the distance in no time, tackled Ferena, and held him until we caught up to Frankie. We got there, beat the guy up some more, but it could have been much worse.

"The incident was meant to send a message to Chris Cognata. Another guy he cannot reach out to for help. Palmaccio made it clear to Ferena, stating, 'Tell Chris we said what's up.' Once we were done, we headed back to Glenpatricks. Palmaccio got even more drunk, and we hung out there for a while, then headed home for the night."

Ronnie G had received information from Padavona, who, in turn, got the information from Frankie Ran.

Ran was the guy who thought he saw Cognata in Allison Brown's car and almost got an innocent girl killed.

Gene continues, "We did know for a fact that Joe DiGangi was Cognata's friend. Whether or not DiGangi was in any way aiding Cognata, we really had no idea. Frankie Ran's information was suspect, and he was biased, for he was deathly afraid of Cognata and would say anything to get us to move on him.

"Ronnie G was frustrated with the entire situation. Here is a made guy, well-known, feared, respected, connections to the hierarchy of the Bonanno family with a nobody of a guy as a thorn in his side. Ronnie's patience was wearing thin, to say the least.

"Joe DiGangi and I were close friends; he was driving the night Crocker was shot through the throat. But Ronnie G, in his state of mind, believed no one heeded his orders when we put it out on the street to stay away from Cognata. He gave us our marching orders; Joe DiGangi was the next target.

"Joe not only was my friend, he was well liked by all of us. This is another big downside of life in the mob, moving against your friends because your boss tells you to.

"The option to say no does not exist. Objecting too strongly or refusing an order could mean your death. Ronnie G wanted Joe shot, not killed, but shot, a solid message he wanted sent. Those were our orders. Bobby G and I headed out, and with no words spoken between us, we both knew Joe needed to be warned. We gave him a heads-up. I called Joe on his phone and told him, 'Come and meet us, right now!' We met at 207 Park and told Joe, 'Bro, go home, stay in the house. If you get any calls don't go, take no meetings. It will be us, and we will be coming to hurt you.'

"Joe said, 'Why Genie?'

"'Because Frankie Ran said you were with Chris.'

"Joe, now knowing he was a target, reached out to anyone who knew anyone to straighten the problem out. It took Joe two, maybe three, weeks, and his issue was resolved. But some resolutions come at a price.

"Eventually, Joe DiGangi would have to meet Ronnie G and speak to him personally. Ronnie set them up a meeting in a secluded area. Joe had to go or he would be hunted. Terrified for his life, DiGangi met Ronnie, and the problem was officially squashed.

"Evidently Ronnie's plan of going after anyone who aided Chris Cognata was taking a toll. The circle of people around Chris had gotten smaller and smaller, to the point where only family members would help; no one on the street would take his calls, meet with him, or do any kind of business with him. Borrello and the rest of the crew had been hunting Chris and those around him for the past three months. Things would soon be coming to a head."

"Maria Ferone and I were dating for a year and a half. She was a nice girl from the neighborhood, respected family, and a gorgeous girl. Two, three nights a week, Maria would spend the night at my apartment. Frequently, Maria would fall fast asleep in the bed while I would be up late at night watching movies. About two o'clock in the morning, my window breaks at the front of the apartment; I look up and I see a hole in my ceiling. There was a short pause after the bullet struck my ceiling, then in rapid succession, bullets were breaking the window, which was the entire front of my apartment and my bedroom. The bed was actually up against the window. Bullets were also hitting the air conditioner mounted in the wall; I could hear the metallic sounds as the bullets made their way through the air conditioner into the apartment. Instinctively, I grabbed Maria and slid her off the bed and onto the floor where we were safe.

"Initially, I heard no gun fire, just the sound of glass breaking and bullets burying themselves in the structure on my apartment. I probably didn't hear the first few rounds, but once the glass was broken, I heard the shots from the street. The gun fire was coming in rapid succession. Good thing I was on the third floor; the angle from the street made it almost impossible to get hit from someone firing from street level.

The renters on the second floor, having an infant in the apartment, immediately called the police to report the shooting. I had to gather up all the weapons and any other illegal contraband I had in the apartment and give it to someone to hide it somewhere."

The New York Police Department arrived en masse. Seven cruisers and plain clothes arrived. The police already knew Borrello's address and that he was O.C.[9] and a Bonanno associate. Naturally, they asked who did the shooting, and naturally, Gene said he had no idea. Because there was a call, there was evidence of shots fired, and the NYPD were required to do the ballistics. When the police do ballistics, they are able to trace the angles of the bullets and put up strings to recreate the path of the bullets.

Three or four rounds struck the headboard from the rear, exactly where Borrello's head would have been had he been asleep. Maria's mother picked her up to take her home. The cops were there for two hours.

"Not wanting to disturb anyone in my crew at that late hour, I went to sleep in the apartment.

"From this incident, I was now on the law's radar.

"The following week, Alcohol, Tobacco, and Firearms would raid my apartment twice. Once, they found a taser, not bothering to pursue it, for it was a misdemeanor.

"After that, they, the A.T.F., didn't come around anymore. "I called my partner, Bobby G; he came over to pick me up, and we went over to Ronnie G's house. I told Ronnie everything that had happened the previous night. Ronnie was beyond livid. He decisively stated, 'We gotta retaliate right away.'

"I asked, 'Whatta ya want us to do?' I had no idea who to retaliate against; Cognata was hiding outside Howard

---

[9] Organized crime

Beach and moving around in the wee hours of the morning. Ronnie said, 'He wants to bring it to your house, bring it to his girlfriend's house -burn her car.' Bobby G and I had our marching orders. We left to exact some semblance of revenge.

"Gina Puma, Cognata's girlfriend, lived in Old Howard Beach, or Howard Beach adjacent, and we knew exactly where she lived. We arrived at the house about midnight, surveilled the area for a short while, spied Gina's car, an Acura TL, green, two door. The car was parked next to the house. Taking the Gatorade bottle full of gasoline, I poured the gas over the hood and windshield of the vehicle. I lit a book of matches, tossed it on the vehicle, and walked over to Bobby G's car, got in, and we sped off.

"When you torch a car, if it's not immediately extinguished, everything burns-the windshield buckles, and the fire spreads to the interior, growing exponentially.

"This fire was particularly bad, and the blaze from the car had grown large enough to spread to the siding of the house. The fire department got there in time and extinguished the fire before any serious damage was done to the house.

"Bobby G and I headed for the boathouse. Everyone was there. We were talking about the possibilities of our actions, hoping to get Chris to come out of hiding, to make a mistake. In the midst of scheming, Ricky Kessler's phone rings. Who's calling?

None other than Chris Cognata. Ricky puts the phone on speaker, and Cognata starts talking trash with everybody present, and the trash talk is going back and forth.

"Then Cognata asks, 'Is Ronnie there?'

"Ricky said, 'Yeah.' Everyone went quiet to allow Ronnie G to talk. Cognata cocks a pistol into the phone so we could hear and then says to Ronnie G, 'I know where your kids go to school; I'm gonna kill 'em.'

"With this statement, Ronnie G shifted gears. Usually, we speak at normal levels; now, Ronnie's voice was hushed and serious -deadly. Ronnie said, 'That's it, we gotta kill this guy.' Ronnie went on to explain that he would work on getting Cognata's location. Ronnie would go to Cognata's uncle, Joe Cavalcante. Ronnie pressured him to give up Cognata's location.

"Joe Cavalcante was an associate of the Lucchese crime family, so he knew the score; he was between a rock and a hard place. To protect his nephew, who threatened a made man's kids on the one hand, over the request of a highly feared and notorious wiseguy on the other was an impossibility. Cavalcante knew if he didn't cooperate with Ronnie G, he would never become a member, for Ronnie G could have a Lucchese member block Cavalcante from getting straightened out. Ronnie could also have Uncle Vin intervene, as the consigliere, even from another family, wielded too much clout to overcome. Uncle Joe gave up his nephew. He provided Ronnie G with the location where Chris Cognata was hiding.

Ronnie learned that Chris was staying with his Uncle Sal Cavalcante in Lindenwood, and he got the address. The address was a remodeled house converted to a three-apartment residence: basement and first and second floors.

"Finally, we had a specific place to watch; we knew the approximate times he was moving around the city. It would be just a matter of time.

"Ronnie G, true to his word, got to the location with a work car and two guns: a Beretta nine-millimeter for me, and he gave Bobby G a Colt .38 Special revolver. He had also formulated an entire plan. The 'work car' was not reported stolen...yet, so we could drive the car without the added concern of the police looking for a stolen car.

"My guess is Ronnie had someone in a garage where the car would be left for several days and reported stolen only if need be. Should we get Cognata, we were to drive the car a short distance and make our way to Ronnie's car where he and Padavona would be waiting to spirit us away.

"The first night, Bobby G and I were unarmed; we were to do surveillance only, to get a feel for the area in case things didn't go to plan. Ricky Kessler had brought a black Pontiac Grand Prix sedan with tinted windows to Ronnie G's house. Bobby G and I went to Ronnie's around eleven o'clock at night to pick up the car. We stopped in to see Ronnie before we left.

"He gave us brief instructions. I was to drive, Bobby G was in the passenger seat, Ricky Kessler was in the back seat, and we were to drive to Lindenwood to wait for Cognata. We found the address and parked a couple of car lengths from the house on the opposite side of the street. It was approximately eleven-thirty at night when we parked, and we took a good, hard look of the neighborhood to get a sense of where to run if we had to. We stayed there in the car for hours waiting, waiting, waiting. We were there until two, maybe three, o'clock before we left. We never saw Cognata.

"The three of us drove back to Ronnie G's house to return the car; he was already there waiting. That's one thing I gotta say, Ronnie was a gangster through and through. He could have easily told us drop off the car and say, 'I'll see you tomorrow.' Nope he was right there.

"The second night, Bobby G, Ricky, and I headed over

to Ronnie G's house. This time, things were a little different. Ronnie had given me the .38 Colt and gave Bobby G the nine-millimeter Beretta. In painstaking detail, he walked all of us through the plan, step-by-step, making certain everyone knew their job.

We would take up the same position as the previous night.

"Should we shoot, we were to drive to a predetermined location, park the car, and the three of us were to walk over to Ronnie G's car where he and Padavona would be waiting. They would get us out of the area. Later, someone would pick up the Grand Prix, and it would be crushed. All five of us were amped up-this would be the deed where Bobby G and I would get proposed for membership. We headed out.

"We took our position until three or four o'clock in the morning. It was a complete repeat of day one. Day three, all of us headed out about the same time, eleven o'clock at night. Arriving on site, we took up our position, but this time, parked further down the street. A precaution, just in case someone had previously seen a suspicious car. After being there for several hours Bobby G, Kessler, and I were ready to call it quits for the night.

"Excitedly, Bobby G says, 'That's him, right there!' Cognata was coming out of the front door. He crossed the street and was walking towards a Dodge Ram 1500. We knew that it was his uncle's truck. For a moment, we thought it was one of the other tenants from the building. Shortly after Cognata had emerged, we were supposed to jump out of the car and gun him down on the spot.

Cognata was being hunted; he was armed and would be alert. Had we ran up on him, there may have been a shootout on the sidewalk at three in the morning. One of us could've been shot, or Cognata could've walked away unscathed. Neither was acceptable.

"We called an audible; his truck was nearly one hundred feet away, parked in a dead-end street. The three of us were shouting out ideas as quickly as they came to us. We had it! I would drive towards Cognata, he wouldn't notice us the windows were tinted, we pass him, make a right onto the deadend street going to the end, make a U-turn, and we would be on the same side of the street. The Ram was parallel parked. Bobby G would have an ideal shot at the driver ---Cognata.

"It worked, the timing was perfect; when I made the U-turn, I saw Cognata nearing the Ram and adjusted my speed so the Grand Prix would be directly alongside the Ram truck with Cognata in the driver's seat. A sitting duck for Bobby G.

"Bobby G was in the passenger seat, putting him literally three feet from Cognata. Armed with sixteen rounds to unload on this guy, Bobby froze. When confronted with actually killing Cognata, he couldn't pull the trigger. I was telling him when the Grand Prix came to a stop in a hushed voice, 'Shoot, now, now, now!' Bobby leaned back in the seat, gun in his right hand and crossed his arm over his body with the gun coming to rest on his chest.

"I acted instinctively when Bobby took no action. Picking up the snub-nosed .38, I leaned over Bobby, held the car in place with my foot on the brake, my arm extended out the window, and fired. I emptied the weapon into the driver's side door and window.

"When the gun went silent, Cognata had slumped over the steering wheel. Bobby and Ricky were excitedly yelling, 'You got 'em, you got 'em.' I recovered, grabbed the wheel, and sped off. As soon as I came to a stop sign and the car came to a standstill, without warning Bobby opened the door and took off running. Kessler in the back seat, same thing. They both jumped out and took off running in different directions.

"I drove to the predetermined destination, parked, got out, and went over to Ronnie's car with Padavona in the driver's seat. Opening the rear door, I get in and tell Ronnie, 'We got him.' Kessler and Bobby were telling me, 'You got 'em.'

"Ronnie asked, 'Where are Bobby and Ricky?'

"I replied, 'They're gone.' "Ronnie said, 'What?'

"I said, 'Gone. When I came to a stop, they both jumped out and ran.'

"After the mass exit by my co-conspirators in the shooting, what remained went to plan. Ronnie said, 'Give me the gun.' I handed him the gun. Padavona started the car, and we drove to

Ronnie G's house. Even though it was between three and four in the morning, I figured Kessler or Bobby would call one of us to check in and make sure everything was all right.

"When we settled in, I gave Ronnie G and Padavona a detailed account of what happened. After a lot was said and done, based on what I saw, what Kessler and Bobby G said, I believed Cognata was dead, but I did not know for sure. We would have to wait for confirmation.

"Nick "Pudgie" Festa would come over to Ronnie's the following morning with an account of what occurred.

"Pudgie had gone over to Ronnie G's house and told him the word on the street was Cognata was not shot, his younger cousin was shot. Pudgie also explained to Ronnie there was only six shots fired, a few of the bullets had gone into the door and a few into the ceiling of the truck. Ronnie G was confused by a couple of things. He was curious why there was only six rounds fired, when there should have been twenty plus rounds fired. Second, this was the first instance of the mention of the younger cousin.

"Evidently, Kessler had gone to Ronnie's house the next day and given him a detailed account of what happened. That was the first time Ronnie would hear that Bobby G had frozen and never fired a shot. Up to that point, I had not mentioned that Bobby never fired; it was assumed that Bobby G had emptied his gun along with me.

"Ronnie G called me and told me to come over. When I got there, Ronnie was there by himself. He started by saying Cognata was not shot, his cousin was. Then the questions started. 'How many times did you shoot?'

"I answered, 'I emptied my gun.' "'What about Bobby?'

"I played it off, shrugged, and tried to evade the question. Ronnie said, 'I already know, you're not rattin' your friend out.'

"I then said, 'He didn't shoot.'

"Ronnie never mentioned the cousin. We assumed it was propaganda Cognata was spreading. Between Kessler, Bobby G, and I spending hours surveilling the residence, one of us would have seen the cousin Cognata was saying got shot.

"Cognata literally dodged a bullet; he would live to fight another day. After this, he was nowhere to be found; events as they unfolded would further work to his advantage.

"Within weeks, Cognata would violate parole and go to jail during September of 2006. Ronnie G would plead guilty to extortion of a stock brokerage firm, be sentenced to seven and-a-half years during November, 2006. And I pleaded guilty to gun possession and reckless endangerment because I tried to shoot a guy for hitting my father in the head with a hammer. I received three to six years in New York State Penitentiary. I went away during December, 2006."

2006 was a violent, tumultuous year where criminal careers were broken and established; the hierarchy of the Bonanno crime family was looking at several crew members to propose for membership, and ultimately be made made men.

LIFE WITH VIN

Time was moving incomprehensibly fast for Gene Borrello. To him, it seemed like just yesterday, he was putting on a tuxedo to go to Bobby G's wedding. That was over a year ago; it was now November, 2011, and Genie was closing in on his second Christmas since coming home. Ronnie G was going to be away almost another year and a half. While Ronnie was away, Gene would continue reporting to Uncle Vin.

Vin was a true Mafia character. He was seventy-six years old, still played paddle ball, was sharp as a razor, full of vim and vigor, still a ladies' man, and loved to gamble. Specifically, he liked going to the track and betting on the ponies. At one time, Vin was worth millions from his work in the life, but he would lose most of his wealth at the track. Vin's was tall, six-feet-plus, around two hundred pounds, with a full head of hair. Of all people, he looked like the actor from Jaws, Roy Scheider.

He had been inducted into La Cosa Nostra in the sixties. There was no telling what information he kmew. Vin literally knew where all the bodies were buried and who put them there.

Gene explains more about his boss, "When I was around Uncle Vin, he was a captain in the Bonanno crime family. Because of his longevity, his knowledge of Mafia life was extraordinary. So much so that other captains would seek his advice and guidance. Once Joe Massino, the boss, would become an informant, the hierarchy of the family would often consult Uncle Vin on family matters and potential decisions.

"Life with Uncle Vin, like I said before, was a curse and a blessing. There were a few occasions when I was in complete awe, witnessing other gangsters as they realized who he was and could not hide their facial expressions. During the months Ronnie G was in prison, I would spend many days looking after Uncle Vin. The times with him are fond memories, even the bad times. In retrospect, my thoughts of Vin always make me laugh, for he was a true character.

"Two words can describe Vincent "Uncle Vin" Asaro: vicious and maniac. There were the stories I hear about him going back to the sixties. The stories were told to me from people in the know -my family, who had ties to organized crime, made guys, and Vin's family members that knew me, and so, we became close. While he became a friend or made guy in 1969 at the age of thirty-four for the Bonanno crime family, he was an associate from the fifties. Prior to the official formation of the five Mafia families, there were many families beyond the named five. Those smaller families in and surrounding New York would be absorbed.

The bosses of those families would become captains under one of the five families. The formation of the five families occurred during 1965.

"Prior to that time, Uncle Vin's grandfather was a boss of his own crime family. And his father was also a boss of his own crime family. His lineage made Vin Asaro Mafia royalty. I heard a story about Vin's father, where he made a guy a meal, they enjoyed their dinner together, and Vin's father shot the guy in his head when they were finished. Vin was third generation Mafioso. That cannot be said about many gangsters, and in our world, it's a big deal. With his pedigree, Vin was given a wider berth than the average made member. He might get an outright pass for violating a rule or a mild reprimand, while someone else may get embarrassingly dressed down. Vin was made during 1969 and became a captain during the seventies. I believe when Joe Massino became the boss during the eighties, he appointed Vin as the counselor or consigliere. Over the years, these two Mafioso powerhouses would grow to hate each other. At some point, either Vin stepped down or was demoted from consigliere to captain. Their hatred for each other would work to Vin's advantage. Because Vin was demoted and out of the hierarchical loop, Joe did not confide in Vin during any relevant period. This would put Vin in the clear when Joe Massino would begin cooperating with the government. After a lengthy trial in 2002, Joe Massino would be convicted and sentenced to two concurrent life terms of imprisonment. In 2005, Massino would become a government informant. Joe would testify at Uncle Vin's trial during 2015, but in reality, he had nothing to add, it was just fluff.

"But I'm getting a bit ahead of myself. When Joe Massino got arrested in 2002, Joe appointed 'Vinny Gorgeous' Bosciano as acting boss. Joe Massino, the don of the Bonanno crime family, ruled for over twenty years. He accumulated an illegal fortune of tens of millions of dollars and was sixty years old when he went to prison.

"Vinny Gorgeous's rule as acting don, or boss, would not be as fortuitous. Massino put Vinny Gorgeous up as boss and took him down as boss. Massino would become a cooperating witness against Vinny Gorgeous in 2005. Massino was sick that most of his fortune, accumulated over a lifetime, would be forfeited to the government, or he could not do the time, or both. Only Joe knows the answer. But Joe's information did untold damage to the Bonanno crime family and put Vinny Gorgeous away for life.

"Once Vinny Gorgeous was arrested, the hierarchical membership of the family approached Uncle Vin and asked him to take over the family.

"Uncle Vin had declined. Ronnie G had told me the story. I often wondered how Uncle Vin said no. Was it one of his rants in his high-pitched voice, when he yelled to make a point, or a gentlemanly no, thank you?

"I would visit, check in, or report in with Uncle Vin three to four times a week. While I would spend all day with Ronnie G when he was out, the fact remained Ronnie was in prison for most of my time as a Bonanno enforcer. Actually, I would spend more time with Uncle Vin simply because Ronnie had a

lengthy sentence to serve. When Vin would scold me, he had a purpose -he was teaching tomorrow's generation of friends. To Vin's generation, the vernacular of the day for a 'made guy' was 'friend.' Had Ronnie been out, he would have proposed me for membership, and I would have gotten made.

"But the time I spent with Vin would be educational, for Vin was the embodiment of La Cosa Nostra. The times with him, his antics, tirades, and lessons, were all memorable.

"The first thing was a debt of ten thousand dollars owed to me by Sonny Franzese's grandson. Sonny was of Vin's caliber, old timers, legends, the stuff of Mafioso lore. But the actual debt was from drugs that was fronted, or lent, to the grandson. The guy fucked up the drugs and could not pay the debt. I went over to his house, knocked on the door, and asked to see Sean when a woman opened the door. She said he wasn't home.

"I left my number with the woman and asked her to have Sean call me. I didn't hear a word for a couple of days. Finally, I received a call, not from Sean, though, but from someone allegedly in the Colombo crime family. That was Sonny Franzese's family. Let's call him Anthony, and he said over the phone, 'I wanna meet, bring somebody.'

"This signaled in mob parlance, if you're not a made guy, bring a wiseguy with you to this 'sit-down.' Anthony thought I was some nobody, some wannabe gangster, a poser. We ended the call, agreeing to meet on Crossbay Boulevard in front of a boarded-up Blockbuster Video rental store. Since I'm reporting to Uncle Vin, he's my guy for sit-downs. I go to see Vin, explain to him he has to sit for me. Without hesitation, he says, 'Give me the details.' I explained to Vin the guy was Sonny Franzese's grandson, which made Vin happy. Sonny was a close friend to Vin, at that time, for fifty years. Anyway, I go on to say Sean owes me ten thousand dollars for a loan he was ducking out on. The reality was the money due from Sean was money he owed me for cocaine he had bought. By La Cosa Nostra rules, I cannot sell drugs, and Sean knew this, that there cannot be a 'sit-down' amongst made members to settle a drug debt. That's why I turned the money into loan money by telling Uncle Vin Sean was trying to duck out on paying a loan. Sean was trying to be cute.

"I had asked Uncle Vin to sit for me, and I would give him fifteen hundred dollars for his trouble. The next day, I get a phone call confirming the meet at Blockbuster and the time, sometime during the day. Uncle Vin and I drive over to meet Anthony; he is not there yet, so we get out and wait on the sidewalk. Anthony pulls up in a Nissan Maxima, he gets out of the car, and approaches us, extending his hand to me when he is near. We shake. I can tell Anthony was nervous; he extended his hand to Uncle Vin, and I say, 'This is Vinny.' Anthony's face registered shock. Anthony realized he was meeting with one of the most powerful guys in the Bonanno crime family and a Mafia legend. Uncle Vin said, 'Are you a friend?'

"Anthony replied, 'No.'

"'I can't talk to you, get the fuck outta here,' Uncle Vin blurted.

"Vin was insulted for having to come out to meet a nobody and was pissed off. Essentially, Anthony was impersonating a made member, which could have gotten him killed. Anthony tried to clean up the situation by explaining his guy couldn't come because this was a drug debt. Uncle Vin, raising his voice said, 'It ain't no drug debt, I gave him' -meaning Sean -'the money. Have my money for me by tomorrow.'

"On the inside, Vin knew the deal, that Sean was being slick, and was angry at the attempt. The money was paid the next day.

"When Anthony realized who he was meeting with and also realized he could have gotten killed had he represented himself as a friend, I imagine he laid into Sean pretty good when he got back. I can readily imagine Anthony screaming at Sean, 'Are you fuckin' crazy? Gene brought Vinny Asaro, you could've gotten me clipped. Pay the fuckin' money.'

"Uncle Vin was seventy-seven around that time. He was consigliere, but the irony was that he really couldn't make money. When Asaro came home from prison in 2002 or 2003, the Committee (boss, underboss, consigliere) would not assign him a crew. Their reason was simple and justified. Asaro borrow money from his own guys to put on the street and blew the money at the track. Vinny was a compulsive gambler. At one time, Vin Asaro had residential and commercial properties, owned restaurants, a Carvel[10], and lost it all living the high life: partying, chasing woman, and gambling. But Vin was respected, paid his dues, been a gangster four decades, and the Committee recognized this. When the consigliere spot opened up, Vin would be assigned as the Bonanno Family's consigliere. While he may have been volatile and a compulsive gambler, he would be excellent at providing guidance for the family.

There are few friends alive who can say they knew Carmine "Lilo" Galante. There are fewer who can say they

---

[10] Ice cream franchise

stood before Lilo, the Bonanno boss, to take the oath to become a made member in La Cosa Nostra. Uncle Vin was both. Uncle Vin respected the titles of all other made members because he had to.

But he only truly respected his perception of real gangsters: guys willing and able to fight, to shoot, to kill...in Vin's eyes, these were the only guys who should be called gangsters.

There were only a handful that he looked at with true respect. Amongst these elite gangsters, Vin was truly one of them. But the gangster he respected the most was Gene Borrello's uncle, 'Fat Andy' Ruggiano. They were great friends to one and other and cut from the same cloth.

Vin, even in his old age, didn't slow down or mellow, though he may have gotten meaner or less patient.

Borrello tells the story:

"There was one occasion when a guy insulted his niece, who was in her midto late-forties at the time, when she was picking up her kid at school. Judy had gotten into an argument with a guy over a parking spot. As words were flying back and forth, the guy called Judy a fat bitch.

"Mike Hintze, Judy's husband, told me what had happened. I immediately took the information to Uncle Vin. As expected, Vin's response was, 'Get him.' Make no mistake, I wanted to get the guy myself, I was just as pissed as Vin. Uncle Vin's order set things in motion. Mike Hintze found out who the guy was. Angelo Giuseppe. He further found out his home address. Hintze did his part; now it was my turn.

"Hintze gave me the address, it was in Ozone Park, virtually the same neighborhood. I go park a safe distance away and begin to watch the house. I saw the guy's car in front of the house, an Infinity, so I knew he was home. All day, I watched, and there was no activity. I was there from morning until night. The next day, I arrived at the house about the same time and remained until dusk, and again, no luck.

"By the third day, my patience was wearing thin. The fact that I lasted that long without kicking in the door was a miracle. Good fortune came my way. I didn't know where they came from, but two cable workers were about to enter Angelo's house.

"I jumped out of the car, closed the distance quickly, being behind the cable workers. I actually forced them through the doorway, for Angelo had opened the door. Once inside, Angelo was a few feet away, the telescoping metal baton I had was fully extended. I swung, trying to hit his hand that was resting on the banister. The ball at the end of the baton found its mark. Angelo screamed out in pain -his hand was broken. To his credit, he reached for a nearby baseball bat, realized he was outmatched, and ran. He made it to the kitchen and hid behind his mother, and I said to him, 'God couldn't save you.' And I went at him, but I could not get a good swing at him. His mother was doing her best to protect her son, and by this time, the two cable guys had raced in to get me off Angelo. I had managed to throw him to the floor and to kick him a couple of times, and I was yelling at the cable guys, 'Get the fuck off, don't get involved.' There were too many people around, too much time had passed, and I succeeded in teaching the guy a lesson. As I left the house, I hit the driver's side window with my baton and bent my baton. I might sound like a nut, but it was my favorite baton, and now I'd have to go through the trouble of getting another one.

"There is more I have to say about my favorite baton. When being debriefed, the Assistant United States Attorney identified my baton as an Asp. I responded, 'What the fuck is an Asp?' Everybody laughed at the debriefing session.

"Angelo Giuseppe had connections of his own. It just so happened that his uncle was a captain known as Conrad of the Genovese crime family. A couple of days later, a friend of mine, a Genovese made member, came to talk to me to let me know what was going on. We were talking as friends, and Sal told me they were mad, actually fuming, over what I did the other day.

"Evidently, the incident had been talked about by the hierarchy of the Genovese family. Sal went on to say my name was coming up all over town and they were saying I was a loose cannon. Then Sal told me Barney said I was a 'walking time bomb.' Barney is the Genovese boss. When I heard that, my chest got pumped, my name was being talked about by a big, respected Mafioso. Sal emphasized, telling me how upset they were. They were mostly upset that I went into the house, not that I attacked Angelo. His mother was the sister of Conrad, and I have no doubt they brought the issue to the boss and wanted blood.

"After all was said and done, I told Sal, 'Tell them to talk to Uncle Psycho, have fun with that.' Sal knew I was acting on Uncle Vin's orders, and he knew my comment was made sarcastically as a joke, but it was nonetheless true. Make no mistake. Uncle Vin was a dangerous guy, a cold-blooded murderer, completely ruthless. All too often, he had to be reasoned with by Ronnie or Jerry Asaro from taking the actions he desired. Had everyone listened to Vin all the time, the streets would have been littered with the bodies of people who offended him on a daily basis. As his enforcer, my job was to do what he told me. I was like a gun, and Vin was the trigger.

"While everything I did, when ordered to do so, was correct, the way I went about it was wrong. Had I beat up Angelo, on the sidewalk there would have been no problem. But my impatience had gotten the better of me, and I went into the house. This rambunctiousness would be my curse throughout my Mafia career. My eagerness to please my superiors was a contributing factor and would lead to a reputation as a 'cowboy.' This could be a blessing or a curse. A perfect scenario would be if I had rubbed a guy like Barney Bellomo (acting boss) the wrong way, If he set his mind to killing me, I would be dead. Depending on what I might have done, even Uncle Vin might not be able to save me.

"Uncle Vin was as much of a hothead as me. One time in a local delicatessen in Howard Beach, Uncle Vin had gotten into an argument with another patron. Over what, I have no clue. Vin was always getting into arguments. At some point, the argument escalated to an altercation. Uncle Vin, at seventy-seven years of age, was thrown to the floor by a guy in his early forties. Vin was irate. But to the guy's benefit, Vin had no idea who he was, but things were not over. Though Vin didn't know the guy, the guy found out who Vin was and realized he may be in danger. The guy turned out to be a janitor named Hike.

Hike was from Howard Beach, which had the largest concentration of Mafioso in the country, and he knew somebody he could contact. Fearful, Hike reached out for help, and somehow he was able to get a meeting with a guy named 'Bobby Glasses,' who was the acting boss of the Gambino crime family. Evidently, they talked, and Glasses reached out for Vin. Bobby Glasses happened to be the right guy to go to; he, by chance, was good friends with Uncle Vin. They agreed to a sit-down. Bobby Glasses sat for Mike, Vin sat for me, the dispute was settled, all vengeance was waived. Hike was good.

"About six to eight months after the deli incident, Bobby Glasses got caught in a big mob round-up, over one hundred guys from several organized crime families were arrested. Uncle Vin was watching to see what happened to Bobby Glasses. Vin's blood was still boiling. From the time Bobby Glasses got arrested, over a year would pass before he would be sentenced. Bobby would be sentenced to life imprisonment. He was never coming home.

"Before the ink could dry on the newspaper article, Uncle Vin gave me the sign. His hand by his neck he motioned with all four fingers together, hand pivoting at the wrist, he motioned to me to cut his throat, actually kill him. While motioning Vin said, 'I want him dead.' Uncle Vin took me to where the guy lived and told me everything I needed to know to carry out his order. Think about that for a second. The whole time Bobby Glasses is locked up, Vin is checking out the janitor's house, so when the time came, he could get even. That's one thing I gotta say, with the old-timers, a vendetta lasted a lifetime.

"Learning of Vin's intentions, even I thought murder was extreme. But I had every intention of carrying out the consigliere's commands. It was my job.

"Hearing Vin's instructions, I went to talk to Mike Hintze, my conduit to Ronnie G in prison. I explained to Hintze Vin's order and my intention to carry it out. Hintze's reaction was no surprise. He shook his head side to side mumbling, 'This maniac.'

"I asked him, 'When you seeing Ronnie?'

"Hintze replied, 'This weekend.'

"I said, 'Tell him what this guy wants me to do.'

"But as far as I am concerned, until Uncle Vin says stop, I'm still in motion. I have to prepare to do this hit. Guns were readily available, but I needed to get a rental car and change out the license plate with a stolen plate. The next step was to go to Mike's home and watch his coming and going to see if there was a routine. He worked as a janitor in a building within walking distance from his home. I never stayed around long enough to find out what time he would return. But I did locate a spot just under an overpass to ambush him and make my escape.

"While I was making my preparations, Hintze was at the prison bringing Ronnie G up to speed. As Hintze described Ronnie's reaction to me, it was actually funny. Hintze explained that he gave the news of Vin ordering the hit to Ronnie, and he exploded, 'What? What is he, fuckin' nuts, you can't kill civilians in the middle of the street!' Ronnie could not tell Vin what to do, he doesn't have the rank, all he could do was try to reason with Vin through someone else. Hintze gave me Ronnie's message as soon as he got back from the prison. I would bring the information to Palmaccio to have him talk to Vin. Hintze could in no way speak about a murder to anyone, he could never be in that circle. If Vin knew I mentioned it to Hintze, I could've gotten into big trouble.

"Vin listened to Palmaccio; the killing of a civilian was bad business and bad for business, and there would be a lot of heat. Ronnie's reasoning rung true to Uncle Vin, and he relented. The next day, Vin changed the order to, 'Throw him a beatin',' but gave me very specific instructions to give the guy a message. That was, 'If you ever disrespect our people again, we'll fuckin' kill you.' "I laid in wait by the overpass and carried out Vin's order to the T, beating the guy with a billy club and delivering Vin's message while he was balled up on the ground. Message sent. Talk

of this would remind everyone in the area that the Mafia was alive and well."

MORE UNCLE VIN

Vinny Asaro's personality left a lot to be desired. He was argumentative, very disrespectful, hypocritical of the rules, threw tantrums, threw objects at people, and would work himself into a psychotic rage. Asaro yelled and hollered at everybody constantly, and he made everybody around him uneasy. At the end of the day, no one could tell him anything. He did have a lovable and charming side as well, but just like a five-carat diamond, you got to see it only once in a while. Asaro did have a good sense of humor, and when he was in the mood, he was fun. As much as he ribbed someone, he could take a ribbing. He was comical, cantankerous, and sometimes out of control; in a word, he was a handful.

"Him knowing he had me around if a problem arose, his first thought was, 'I'll call Genie Boy,'" Borrello recalled. "Because I was handling most of the muscle work in Ronnie's crew, plus the fact that I was reporting to Uncle Vin, he knew he would see me in a day or two to give me an order.

"Uncle Vin, Mr. Personality, was driving somewhere, and he got cut off by another driver. The window lowered, and Uncle Vin started arguing with the guy.

"Only God knows what this nut said or what the other driver said to Vin. Whatever it was pushed Vin over the edge. He followed the guy home, took the license plate number of the vehicle.

Later, he gave the tag number to Bam. He was a well-trusted guy in our crew and the owner of an automotive garage, making Bam the right guy to obtain the information from the tag number for Uncle Vin.

"Uncle Vin had already been to the house and knew the layout. At one point, he took me with him, showed me everything, and told me he wanted me to torch the car.

"Okay, I got the order; when, how, and with whom would be up to me. I got two guys to help me: Fat Matt and John Gotti, the grandson of the once boss of the Gambino family. I took a quick ride over to Broad Channel, which was about ten minutes from Howard Beach, to see if the car was at the house. It was. I drove back to Gotti's house, told John we'd use his car, a four-door Jaguar X-Type. Fat Matt got in the back, and I was in the passenger seat. Our first step was to the gas station to get fuel and put some gas into a Gatorade bottle. This would be one more of dozens of arsons under my belt. Murphy's law was in full force; everything that could go wrong went wrong.

"We arrived at the house, it's between two and three in the morning, the car is parked on the street in front of the house. No problem. Gotti pulled over about fifty feet in front of the car. Fat Matt and I jumped out of the car like we're gone shopping, neither of us looked around, and we walked directly to the pick-up truck. I opened the bottle of Gatorade and began to pour the gas all over the hood and windshield. Fat Matt struck a match, lighting the remaining book on fire, and tossed the lit book onto the hood of the truck.

"The truck lit in a plume of flames; it's dazzling, you don't want to turn away, but we gotta get out of the area. As soon as we turn, we were like two deer caught in the headlights of an oncoming car. Just across the street, there is a cop wearing a white shirt, in a plain car, watching us.

"We break into a run. Fat Matt had that nickname for a reason: he was four hundred pounds. "Surprisingly, he was fast. He closed the distance on the Jaguar in no time. Good thing it was a four door, could you imagine this four-hundred-pound guy trying to get into the back seat of a two door? I arrived at the car with Matt virtually at the same time. When I jumped in, I excitedly told Gotti, 'The cops, go, go, do not stop this fuckin' car!' He took off, flooring the gas, already on the Boulevard. It was a straight shot.

"He reached speeds in excess of 100 miles per hour, running red lights. The cop had to make a U-turn, so we had a head start, but he was on us. I told John to make a right. He did, but he was going too fast and lost control of the car and skidded out. He reversed to straighten out to continue, but the cop made the turn as well; he was closing on us. Then I told Gotti, 'I'm gonna jump out.' The car was moving, I jumped out, tucked and rolled, got up, and started running. The cop came after me. I was jumping fences, running through yards. Finally, when I felt safe, I was hiding in someone's yard. I was a mess. My wrist was badly hurt, clothes torn and tattered, scratches on the side of my face, phone screen broken, and the Rolex I wore was terribly scraped. I stayed there for two hours before I felt it was safe to move. My phone still worked, so I called my friend Ray between four and five in the morning, and he came and picked me up.

"Ray wasn't really a criminal, but when we asked him to do simple things, he was reliable. As a tow truck driver for

Bam's, I knew Ray would be on call. He also would listen to the scanner to hear for car accidents -the first tow truck usually got the work.

"Ray had heard the entire car chase as it was being reported by the police car that was in pursuit. When he picked me up and I told him what happened he said, 'That was you?' Ray drove me to my apartment. It was good to be home; what a long fuckin' night. I tended to my wounds as best I could. I probably should have gone to the hospital for my wrist, but it eventually healed on its own.

"The next day, I reported in to Uncle Vin. I never told him what went wrong. Had I, he would have had a fit, and I would have never heard the end of it.

"Uncle Vin knew me socially all my life. Even when I was younger and I began leaning towards a life of crime, I was on Ronnie's and Vin's radar. In my later years, I would do anything they asked for twelve years, including the time I was in prison. Overall, over time, I gained the trust of Ronnie and Vin. The period when Ronnie was away, I became even closer with Uncle Vin. Ronnie had taught or schooled me on the Mafia, but Uncle Vin took it to the next level. Sometimes, though, what Ronnie taught me would conflict with what Vin taught me. Ronnie's schooling would teach me, should anyone put their hands on me, I was to respond accordingly and beat the piss out of them. It didn't matter who they were; touching me was like touching Ronnie, and you don't put your hands on a made guy. Even if I got into a fight with a member, if he hit me first and I fought the guy, win or lose, I'm in the wrong. But Ronnie said he would straighten it out later at a sit-down. Naturally, Ronnie would sit for me, but a decision could come down, and Ronnie may have to serve me up to be killed.

"While on the other hand, Vin taught me just the opposite: you never, under any circumstances, touch a member. Whatever they may have done would be worked out at a sit-down. Vin taught me right. Even within a criminal organization, the sitdown to settle disputes was essential, or there would be anarchy.

"Vin, as consigliere, had to look at situations from a different perspective. Make no mistake, Vin was a violent gangster, but for longevity and continuity, diplomacy was absolutely necessary. Of the younger guys coming up, I was probably closest to him, and he would confide in me. Often, he would tell me, 'you're the future' of the mob. When I would later debrief to the Assistant United States Attorney's Office, this statement would infuriate the officials."

The Mafia that began Sicily, with its men of honor and code of silence and a myriad code of conduct, began in the nineteenth century.

It has served several purposes over those years and has gone through several iterations, as it will again. As long as there are vices, there will be those willing to provide a product. The American Mafia is seemingly in a downcycle, but it will never be totally obliterated so long as there are people with treachery in their souls.

Gene makes this abundantly clear:

"Understanding the longevity of the Mafia helped me comprehend Uncle Vin's desire for its continuity, for it was his life and the lives of his ancestors. While around Vin at that time, he taught me about the administration of the Mafia so I could contemplate its structure."

THE ADMINISTRATION

During the 1950s, the Mafia was massively strong, a national powerhouse. At that time, even J. Edgar Hoover, who founded and ran the F.B.I., hadn't admitted the existence of La Cosa Nostra.

New York City had always been the strongest Mafia city outside of Palermo, Sicily. Estimates of more than five thousand soldiers and of hundreds of made men was not an exaggeration. In addition to the five families, the Commission was formed, which included the heads of the most powerful Mafia families throughout the United States. Vin Asaro was part of those days.

"When I think about this and the fact that Uncle Vin was a part of the formation of the organization, I am awestruck.

"I was reporting to Uncle Vin during Ronnie's absence. I was now his enforcer! As I was being schooled by Ronnie G and Uncle Vin about the rules, there were so many instances when I would witness hypocrisy. I began to second guess La Cosa Nostra. Especially Uncle Vin, he was the worst. Absolute power corrupts absolutely. Let's face it, as a top-ranking Mafioso, you have the authority to order someone's death. Anyone can pull a trigger, but few have the authority to order another to pull that trigger. This is absolute power.

"The top spot is the boss. There are several ways a boss may come to be. The boss of any crime family is chosen by the captains during peaceful times. But a family can be taken by an aggressive captain with a strong crew. Usually in a situation like this, he will have the support of several other captains. Assassinating a boss is a serious matter, and one could be killed should things awry. Usually, the membership is disgruntled. The boss may be too greedy, asking his captains to kick-up too much in their monthly payments, is weak, or is too quick to kill. The Commission can authorize the killing of a boss, and no one would know but the replacement. And lastly, the reigning boss could step down and appoint a new boss -usually it's the underboss.

"Next in succession is the underboss. The underboss is selected by the boss to succeed him or act for him in his absence.

"Below the underboss is the councilor or consigliere to the boss. The consigliere, the number three man, would become acting boss in the event the boss and underboss went to prison, got killed, or for any other possible reason. The consigliere could also be chosen over the underboss by the Commission to replace the boss.

"These three positions represent the hierarchy of any organized crime family. These same positions are also referred to as the panel or the administration. While the boss has the final say, as in any autocracy, oftentimes on the day-to-day decision making, all three will give input. And in some instances, a vote would be taken and a judgment rendered.

"Just below the administration is the captain. The captain will have his own crew comprised of soldiers, and he is responsible for all of them; their actions reflect directly on their captain and the family. An improper action by a crew member or soldier could get himself and his captain clipped. As an example, let's say a soldier brought a new guy around to put him on record, and he turned out to be wearing a wire. Well, the rat and the soldier are supposed to be killed. Should a soldier step too far out of line, his captain may order him clipped, but clearance from the boss is necessary.

"One of the perks of being a captain is getting an envelope from every made member in his crew. The rate is set by the captain. Amongst the Bonanno made guys I was around, they were responsible to pay one thousand per man per month. Jerry Asaro, a Bonanno captain, had approximately ten wiseguys under him. Of the ten thousand a month he was collecting, he would be required to pay an amount set by the boss to be divided by the administration.

"Soldier, made guy, button man, wiseguy, member, friend, and countless other names, is the frontline guy, the backbone of the Mafia. A soldier's responsibilities is loyalty to his family or boss and to fulfill the oath he swore. By no means is he low man on the totem pole. While there is no specific time frame to becoming a soldier, it may take anywhere from five to ten years from the time a guy is put on record. The Genovese crime family is requiring its associates or crew members to serve ten years before becoming a made member. Regardless of the family and time frame, there are no guarantees. During that period, the potential member would be tested in every way imaginable to be certain he conducts himself correctly.

"The day-to-day responsibilities of each soldier varies

greatly. They may have their own shylock operation, sports book, extortion racket, gambling, and any scheme imaginable, to earn money. Or there may be a situation where a soldier is assigned by his captain to oversee some activity; say, to assure an underground casino runs smoothly.

"A soldier may have guys that are 'around' him; they are trusted guys, usually friends he grew up with on the same path. The number of associates is unlimited, but only those that are put on record can one day become members. Outside that circle, a member may see a neighborhood tough coming up, have one of his more trusted guys approach him to have a conversation. He'll see where his head is at, say 'my guy' wants to talk to you. Then the wiseguy would have a conversation with the prospective crew member. Guys can get looked at because they are tough, big earners, scam artists, or dangerous; all types are needed to fill the ranks of a criminal organization, and everyone has their area where they shine. One guy may be scared to death to steal but be thorough as an armed robber.

"Associates, the guys soldiers rely on, are of two types: those who are not on record and those who are on record. The latter of the two are potential candidates to one day becoming a soldier. But there is more to it than that; once you are put on record, you are recognized by the family, and you must act accordingly. Essentially, each crew member is attached to and subordinate to a soldier, and, frequently, is also attached to a crew. A soldier may have any number of 'guys' in his crew under him, and they answer to their wiseguy. The quality of a soldier's crew is what will get him recognized by his captian, and possibly the administration, for quality 'guys' make a wiseguy powerful. When the higher-ups see this, they will see that soldier as a future crew leader or captain.

"A perfect example of a soldier par excellence was Ronnie G. He had ten associates that I knew of, but more importantly, Ronnie G became a multimillionaire from loans and sports. His only other source of income was 37,000 dollars from some job. It is estimated he earned three-and-a-half million dollars per year. To make that kind of money in loans and sports action is an unheard of achievement.

"The crew member not put on record is a different animal altogether. Naturally, there are the guys who are brought in by guys on record, and once the wiseguy is satisfied, they may be put on record.

"But there are others who will never be put on record. The other guys know it, and the wiseguy is well aware that he will never put a particular guy on record with his captain. These guys are basically gophers, and there's not much else to say.

"Then you have wannabes. These are the guys paying a wiseguy like Ronnie G a nice monthly stipend to hang around with him. To tell other people, 'Hey, I'm good friends with Ronnie G,' but making such a statement without approval could get you a beatin'. On the flip side, saying you know a notorious gangster will get you protection and possibly instill fear in a person who doesn't know any better. But let this schmuck say this to the wrong guy, and he is getting the short end of the stick, no matter what.

"There is one quick story worthy of mentioning; it's ridiculous. Joe DeLucia owned a medium-sized construction company, and I liked Joe. He was the general contractor on Ronnie's new home construction project. Ronnie mentioned to Joe that he was on parole, and he asked Joe to put him on the books so Ronnie would be employed. Joe agreed. Mistake. Joe ended up paying Ronnie G fifteen hundred a week for a no-show job.

"One day, Ronnie G and I were in his truck, and I was on speakerphone telling Bones the story Ronnie just told me. I told Bones, 'Ronnie found a new victim, he's walkin' around his house, get ten paid for it .'

"That should give you a good idea of how an organized crime family operates. Though I am most familiar with the Bonanno family ,the structure is the same in all the families, and all families have rules that are to be followed. Some rules are universal, while others will be unique to that family. I don't know all the rules, but there is an extensive list I am familiar with.

"The three top rules that, if violated, warrant you being killed are: ratting, stealing from the family and selling drugs. A simple example is: a guy picks up a thousand dollars and delivers eight hundred to a member because he thinks no one will ever know. If he gets found out, he will be killed. And, to sell drugs is an offense that warrants death; yet everyone sells drugs, and the rule is seldom enforced.

"No homosexual activity. A killing offense, and no one is

getting a pass.

"Always side with a friend, no matter what. If you don't, it warrants a reprimand and possibly a beating.

"Do not hurt a civilian, women, or children. The punishment would be determined based on the offense by the panel.

"Do not sleep with a member's girlfriend or wife. "No embarrassing the family. An associate or member will avoid any conduct that would put the family in a

bad light. For example: one made guy was posing shirtless on Instagram -modeling, attempting to meet women. They talked about killing him, but put him on the shelf for six months.

"A member cannot be killed without permission. "Violation is death. "One member cannot put his hands on another member.

"Punishment would be determined by the hierarchy.

"A boss cannot be killed without permission. Only the Commission can order a boss killed. A coup would warrant the death of the conspirators.

"But, the successful coup of an unpopular boss may be forgiven. All these rules, though not all inclusive, are not hard and fast, nor applied evenly. Like any bureaucracy, it becomes less about the just application of laws or rules and more about who violated the rule. Where if an unpopular soldier sleeps with another member's wife and gets caught, he will be killed. Let it be a popular member, a big money earner, and he will get a reprimand. Other members would be coming forward to say the woman was a slut, she sleeps with everybody. Hypocrisy permeates every facet of life in America where there is bureaucracy; there is no reason to think organized crime would rise above it."

CRIME NEVER TAKES A HOLIDAY

When Mafioso's money was at risk or there became a growing fear of informants, especially when there was a high-profile crime or big money at risk, people started dying, for the government knew that by applying enough pressure and finding the right candidate, someone would cooperate. The domino effect began; one informant led to the next and so on. Between the state of New York and the federal government, Gene Borrello's life of crime would be put on hiatus. This was not to say things didn't go on from behind bars. Being a gangster or an associate in jail simply meant that you carried yourself in a certain way, demanding a certain level of respect and confidence. A gangster was a gangster at all times.

Oftentimes, violence was required because the mob guy couldn't go back to the streets being known as a pushover. There was more gossip on a prison block than on the reality show, The Real Housewives of New Jersey. Whatever happened in prison was going directly to the streets faster than a speeding bullet.

Prison life broke down to race first, and this was much more prevalent in prison than it was on the streets. As soon as a guy goes in, he would gravitate toward his own kind.

Italians usually cliqued up immediately, and it was just like the streets in an organizational pecking order. The made guys, associates, the wannabes, and then the unaffiliated. Regardless of "rank," everybody had to watch each other's back. Strength was truly in the numbers in jail.

Borrello explains in his own words, "When I violated my probation, I pleaded guilty and was sentenced to 3-6 years. I was sent to Groveland, New York State Correctional Facility, a medium-security institution.

"Like everyone else, I was assigned to a unit. When I hit the yard, I sought out other Italians. There were very few Italian guys there from the burroughs. Finally, I met Angelo from the Bronx; he was doing 12-25. Angelo had machine-gunned a guy in his neighborhood. He and I were alike in many ways. We would hang out every day, but we were in different units.

"After being there for six months, I had gotten into a fight with a guy for owing me money. I received forty days segregation time. While I was away, a guy named Frank Pasqua hit the compound. As soon as I got back, Angelo told me another Italian was in the compound. I was playing handball when a guy came up to me saying, 'Are you Gene?'

"'Yeah,' I answered "'From Howard Beach?' "'Yeah.'

"'I'm Frankie from Staten Island. Who you know from Howard Beach?'

"'I know everybody,' I blurted

"'You know Ronnie Giallanzo?' Frank queried "'That's my direct circle.' I quipped.

"Frankie caught on to my cryptic statement and realized straight away I was either a made guy or around one. We talked more, and I learned his father was a made member for the Lucchese crime family. And Frankie, like me, was in a crew, we were fast friends and inseparable from that point forward.

"It was mid-2008. Angelo, Frankie, and I were together every day. We genuinely enjoyed each other's company. Clowning around, watching each other's back, though the prison was fairly laid back, not much violence. The inmate who worked Receiving and Discharge came and told us another Italian guy just arrived. The following day, we meet the guy on the yard. We introduced ourselves, and he responded telling us he was Sal Giolondo. Sal was from the Bronx, but originally, he was from Howard Beach.

"Before Sal had gotten to Groveland, the three of us had a lot of sway in the yard. Frankie and I had plenty of cash being sent from the street, and we spread it around. Angelo wasn't as fortunate, but he was with us and was a good guy and a loyal friend to Frankie and me.

"We had been talking with Sal for nearly a month,

but none of us ever mentioned that Frankie and I were connected. Sal, originally from Howard Beach, would constantly drop names of people he allegedly knew. He was talking like he was in the life, but in reality, he was a nobody, a wannabe. Sal didn't appreciate the influence Frankie and I had at the prison. He started talking about us behind our backs, telling people we were 'piss-ons,' nobodies, peons. Sal wanted to be the 'guy' by taking us down and putting himself up.

"Because of the influence we had, another Italian guy from

upstate New York was loyal to us, came to tell us what was going on. Nobody wanted to say anything because they did not want to cause a problem, but I appreciated the guy telling us. Once we heard, Frankie and I talked about what we should do. I really didn't want Frankie doing anything because Frankie was a huge, strong guy, six foot, two inches, three hundred pounds. Strong as a bull. Whatever we decided, we could not get caught.

"We didn't act straight away. Then we found out Sal was talking about some Gambino guys from Ozone Park. I called Burga; he happened to be at the social club where everybody was hanging out. I asked if anybody knew a guy named Sal Giolondo. Burga had put me on speaker. Al Trucchio, a captain with the Gambinos, yelled out from the back of the club, 'He's no good,' indicating Sal was a rat. Not good for Sal. After we thought about, it we figured Sal wanted to discredit us before we found out about him and put the word out that he was a rat.

"Knowing this, I wanted to have someone lure Sal to a blind spot in the institution, where we would cover our faces and give him a beating. Nope. Frankie being Frankie wanted to cut him. We did everything as planned. Sal was lured to a dark spot, we had scarves wrapped over our faces, I punched Sal in the head, and Frankie cut his face with a tin can lid. Sal knew it was us, and he told the administration. Frankie took the weight, telling the staff I had nothing to do with it; it was all him. He received one year in segregation and one year loss of good time.

"Frankie taking the weight was proof of his loyalty to our bond and friendship. He would be transferred to Clinton State Penitentiary, a particularly bad joint. During the latter part of 2009, Frankie would meet, of all people, Chris Cognata. Frankie knew all about Cognata and knew he was my and Ronnie G's enemy. At his core, Frankie was Mafioso. There was an underlying loyalty to our way of life. Cognata had been at Clinton before Frankie got there. Like any other joint, Frankie was the new Italian guy. Cognata approached him and asked where he was from. Frankie told him Staten Island. Cognata volunteered the information that he was from Howard Beach. Frankie already knew who Cognata was and that he was a problem. Frankie asked Cognata, 'You know a guy named Gene?'

"Cognata replied, 'Yeah, he's a blowjob.'

"Frankie added, 'He's a jerk-off, I was just with him at Groveland.'

"Cognata invited Frankie to join him and his friends in the yard.

"That afternoon, Frankie was already in the yard when Cognata came out. Frankie had spoken to the Italians in the yard to get clearance to go after Cognata. He explained that Cognata had threatened to kill a wiseguy's kids; specifically, Ronnie Giallanzo. When Frankie said that, he could've asked to kill Chris, and they would have given their blessing. Obviously, they gave him the go-ahead. When Cognata hit the yard, he approached Frankie saying, 'What's up?' Frankie waited until he was close enough to reply to Cognata's greeting with a head butt. Followed up with a barrage of punches, they wound up rolling around, getting broken up, and they were both put in the hole.

"Problems with people just don't go away. Sal Giolondo, the guy Frankie and I beat up at Groveland, tried to set me up. I had been transferred from Groveland to Green Correctional, and Sal had been released. Giolondo sent a package of heroin, concealed in an envelope, to me, trying to get me charged. There was an internal investigation by the prison administration. While they could not prove it was a set-up, they knew the dope was not mine, and the investigation was concluded.

"After all this nonsense in prison, my four years I had to serve was up. I was released July 16, 2010.

"I had known months in advance what my release date from prison was; it just so happened to be the same day my closest friend Bobby G was getting married. Being away three years and seven months was in a whole different craziness. I was sliding right back into the swing of things...like I never left.

"Green Correctional was two-and-a-half hours from home. My mother and Aunt Connie had picked me up. Naturally, I was happy to be free, but in reality, it didn't seem like I was gone long. I had stayed in touch, knew what was going on in the streets, had gotten regular visits, and had plenty of money. I was allowed to receive thirty-five pounds of food per month. I would receive extra by finding one or two guys who didn't have anything and have my family send them a package, giving them ten pounds out of the package; it was a win-win. Some of the guys I was around were doing well for prison.

"Once we got home, my mother dropped me off on Crossbay Boulevard. All my friends were there, waiting.

Hugs all around; it was great to be home amongst my element. I told the guys, 'I gotta go get ready for a wedding.' I don't think I believed what I

had just said. No haircut, still have the smell of prison on me. The more I thought about it, I just wanted to get to my apartment, shave, shower, and dress in some descent clothes. My mother had rented me an apartment in Lindenwood and furnished it for me. Bobby G had arranged everything in the apartment, stocked it with anything he thought I might want. When I finished showering Bobby had bought me a tux for his wedding; I was in the bridal party. This was surreal: released at eight that morning, and several hours later, I'm in Bobby G's bridal party."

Crime, like death, never took a holiday. Ronnie G was in prison and was scheduled to be released in April, 2013. While waiting for Ronnie G, Borrello reported to Uncle Vin Asaro and started reporting on his second day home from prison.

"I never thought twice about it; to not be around these guys would have been abnormal...I loved the life, and I was back.

"I was reporting to Uncle Vin because Palmaccio and Ronnie G were having some problems with each other, and Ronnie didn't want me around Palmaccio. I asked Uncle Vin if I should talk to Palmaccio because we're all together. Vin said, 'Don't get involved,' implying it's made guy bullshit, solely between them. While I was in this crew and an enforcer for Ronnie G and Uncle Vin, it was an in-house matter and not my place to intervene.

That said, no matter what, Ronnie G was my guy, and I was with him to the end."

Checking in with Vincent "Uncle Vin" Asaro was a curse and a blessing. Vin was the consigliere of the Bonanno crime family, the number three man. The family had been offered to him at one time, and he passed on the opportunity to be boss. But by the time Tommy DiFiore took over as boss in 2012, they had to convince Vin to take the number three spot. He was wanted because he was old Mafioso, knew the rules and how to run a family. DiFiore, for all intents and purposes, was a rookie compared to Uncle Vin.

Borrello expands on his interim position, "The blessing of reporting to Uncle Vin was that any trouble I got into, barring some serious violation of La Cosa Nostra rule, Vin was taking my side. As the consigliere, the only guys Vin answered to were the underboss and boss; everybody else was under him. In that respect, I had carte blanche. But the curse was also due to his rank -when Uncle Vin said something, he meant it. Vin at that time was seventy-five and sharper than guys half his age, and I loved him.

"When I finished with Vin, I had to go check in and see Mike Hintze, Ronnie G's brother-in-law. Hintze had been doing Ronnie's collections while he was away, and people were taking advantage of Hintze. I went to see him the second day out of prison, and the first thing he gave me was the deadbeat list -all the guys stiffing him on their weekly payments. Once we settled that issue, I needed to start earning immediately. When word spread that I was out, guys would want to borrow and start handling my sports book again. Hintze was handling all of Ronnie's finances as far as loans. It would take me a month to get up and running again, but the action and cash flow would grow exponentially. While meeting with Hintze, he had told me the last time he went to visit Ronnie G at the prison, Ronnie told him emphatically, 'Watch him, ya gotta watch him, or it's gonna be chaos.' Hintze was too busy and a pushover, ergo the lengthy deadbeat list.

"Okay, I checked in with Uncle Vin, took care of future business prospects with Hintze. I had a little time to myself. When my mind slowed, I could not help but think about the problems between Palmaccio and Ronnie G. It was eating at me. After talking with Hintze, Bobbie G, and Padavona, I got a pretty good idea what was going on between these guys. It started with Palmaccio cursing out Ronnie G's sister for some reason, then escalated from there. Palmaccio had 150,000 dollars on the street for Ronnie G at one point, the vig being fifteen hundred a week. Palmaccio made a move to put a little more money in his own pocket while Ronnie was in prison. He went to their captain, Jerry Asaro, Uncle Vin's son, to tell him how much money Ronnie had screwed him out of on his monthly payments. Ronnie was supposed to pay his captain a thousand a month.

"But Ronnie tricked Palmaccio, telling him he had to pay two thousand a month; Palmaccio was paying a thousand for himself and Ronnie's end. Now it was Palmaccio's turn. He told Jerry that Ronnie was getting a hundred thousand a month for shaking down the brokerage firm, plus his weekly sports book and loan shark money, which was about thirty to fifty thousand a week. Ronnie was supposed to kick up about ten percent. Jerry would have taken five percent because the numbers were so large.

"Jerry was pissed. The150,000 dollars Ronnie had on the street, no more vig payments, the amount would be 'knocked down,' and Ronnie would receive five hundred a week, meaning what payments Palmaccio received came off the principal of the loan until it was paid off completely. And regardless of what Palmaccio received, Ronnie got five hundred. Jerry justified this by sending Ronnie a message telling him, 'You got enough money.' Jerry's action were an insult of the highest order, but in retrospect, Ronnie deserved it for being so greedy.

"Jerry Asaro was Ronnie G's first cousin, and I am guessing Ronnie felt he could get away with a mere thousand a month. Ronnie G was a great guy in every respect, save one; when it came to money, he was ravenous. Anything his guys did on their own, without Ronnie's involvement whatsoever, he still expected a kickback of ten percent. A perfect example was when Pudgie would do the fireworks sale on July 4th.

He would get an illegal shipment of fireworks, maybe a hundred thousand dollars' worth, put on a fireworks show in the neighborhood, and sell the rest to make a profit. Good for the community and good for business. I would guess Pudgie would make fifty thousand profit. Ronnie knew Pudgie did this every year. Well, one year, Pudgie forgot to give Ronnie an envelope for three or four days past the fourth. By the second day, Ronnie kept asking me, 'Gene, you see Pudgie.' I knew what it was about, and I saw the pus on Ronnie's face when Pudgie did not show up. I gave Pudgie a heads-up, telling him, 'Ronnie's waiting for the fireworks money.' Pudgie was like, 'Are you serious?' Pudgie was making Ronnie forty thousand a month, yet Ronnie was chomping at the bit to get a few thousand from Pudgie. Ronnie had no problem taking money for nothing and every problem with kicking up to his captain.

"Had Ronnie pulled that bullshit with any other captain, there was a very good chance he would have been killed, and everything he had would have been taken for being cheap to his captain. So, this problem between Palmaccio and Ronnie was going on, and I was with Ronnie, I felt I had to protect Ronnie and his interests, regardless of his bad ways.

"Within my first week out of prison, I was on the phone with Palmaccio. The call was by no means congenial. I told Palmaccio we could meet right now, him and me, just us, nobody has to know. Well, we never fought, and Palmaccio told Uncle Vin on me.

"Uncle Vin called for me the next day, and I had to go meet him at a local delicatessen where Vin held court. He did not ease into conversation, it wasn't his way. Vin started hollering like a maniac immediately, 'Who the fuck you think you are?' And he continued on with his tirade. I blanked out; I was used to his rants and ravings. I do remember him saying, 'Stay out of it.' I tried to explain to Vin, no matter what, I was going to protect Ronnie, and I did not like what Palmaccio was doing while Ronnie was away in prison and helpless. At the end of the day, it was between two made guys and not my affair. Vin couldn't have been that mad at my attempted intervention because he didn't throw anything at me.

"Yep, when I pushed Vin a little too far, he would resort to throwing things. On one occasion, it was the son of a Lucchese member. The kid went to his father, the father complained to Vin, and I get a loaf of bread thrown at me when he had his tantrum.

"Vin was putting on a show for Frankie 'Cat,' the kid's father. They were friends, and in reality, I knew that Frankie Junior's father was made. By the rules, I'm supposed to go to the father to resolve the problem.

"My concern for Ronnie G was not just because he was my guy; in my eyes, he was my peer. I saw us as equals in all respects for many, many reasons. Amongst our own crew, I took a leadership role; it came naturally. For some reason, guys just seemed to listen to me. In the neighborhood, I was well liked, but more importantly, I was respected and feared. Because of all my activities: shootings, beatings, arsons, et cetera, made guys from other families believed I was a made member. Oftentimes, I would talk with these guys, and they automatically assumed I was a wiseguy during our conversations. I would have to correct them, telling them 'not yet.' But I knew I was on the fast track to getting my button. Actually, right after the attempted murder of Chris Cognata, had Ronnie and I not gone to prison, he would have proposed me, and I would have become a member.

"Getting back to Hintze and the first order of business, he proposed the deadbeat list and its biggest offender, Brian Fahey. Ronnie had passed word to Hintze to tell me to go to Fahey's manual car-wash and detailing business and give him a beating if he didn't pay. I asked my friend Adam to come with me. When Fahey saw me walking up with Adam, all the blood drained from his face; he was white as a sheet. Before I could say a word, Fahey said, 'Gene, we can't do anything here, I'm being watched by the feds.' This was nothing but a half-a-rat move to avoid a beating. Fahey was smart; he knew I just came home from prison and would be on parole. And it worked...for the time being.

"So I told him, 'Listen, I was supposed to give you a beatin', but you had me go back. Just pay Ronnie what you owe him.' Fahey had borrowed seventy-five thousand from Ronnie at one point, so the vig was seven hundred and fifty dollars a week, and he had missed several weeks by the time I went to see him.

"Brian started making payments to Hintze for a couple of weeks and then disappeared. He lived in Middle Village, Queens, so unless he left New York all together, we would find him. For the seventy-five thousand and what he owed Ronnie, we would not stop looking anytime soon, if ever. Odds were that Fahey would be back to Queens in the near future. We would put word on the street; as soon as he was back, someone would give us a heads-up.

"In the meantime, I got about twenty thousand from Ronnie at one point. I would put it on the street at three points. On the two points net, I would get four hundred in vig. Not much, but I was rebuilding my loan shark action and my sports book.

"The reality was simple: Hintze could not handle Ronnie's business the way Ronnie wanted him to. Ronnie was a very aggressive guy, and Hintze was the polar opposite. Basically, Hintze was doing Ronnie a favor while he was away. For all of Hintze's trouble, Ronnie bought him a Ford F-150 truck for twenty-seven thousand dollars. Hintze was collecting about thirty thousand a week, and Ronnie was going to be away for seven years. Ronnie was grossing one point five million a year while incarcerated. He was gradually getting Hintze to back off the deadbeats and have me take over. Ronnie wanted me doing collections because I was aggressive like him. My role as Ronnie's enforcer worked quite well in these situations. Also, it became clear my role as Ronnie's and Vin's enforcer would become solidified during Ronnie's incarceration.

Three, maybe four, weeks after I was home, I got a call from Ronnie, from prison. The first thing he said: 'Thank God you're home. I got nobody on the street for me.' The rest of his crew wasn't trustworthy, others not capable or reliable, and other guys were either in prison or on supervised release or parole. While I was on parole, I had no problem tending to Ronnie's affairs. At the end of the day, I was a criminal through and through -you find a way around a problem or you go through it.

"Hintze and I were doing weekly collections for Ronnie G while he was in prison. He had three million on the street. We collected thirty thousand dollars a week. Ronnie gave me balls, nothing, nil, for the work. I got to borrow money at one point and would lend it at three points. If Hintze had any problems with collections, we would move that name onto my collections list.

"One name that ended up on my list once again was Brian Fahey's. This guy was slick; once I talked to him at the car-wash, he paid Hintze for several weeks. But he started missing payments once again. This had gone on for a couple of months. Hintze didn't want to say anything because he did not want to come off as incapable or weak. At one point, Fahey had called Hintze to tell him to meet him at a specific place so he could pay him. Fahey never showed. When Hintze went to visit Ronnie and told him what happened, Ronnie told him to have me shoot at him to give Fahey a good scare.

"The next time I saw Hintze, which was fairly regularly, he gave me the message. Actually, I was looking forward to shooting at Fahey; he was pulling some real bullshit. I had a snub-nose Colt .38 Special, and after I thought about Fahey, had I 'accidentally' shot him and he died, it wouldn't have mattered. First, I went to his hand car-wash and detailing service and watched him closing up the business. I knew where his apartment was, so I would go there and wait for Fahey to show up. After a couple of minutes in the car, I got out to wait by the side of his building. Fifteen to twenty minutes later, I was freezing. It was November, 2010, and we were having a cold winter, so I got back in my car. Just after I got in the car, I see Fahey pulling up. Wanting to walk up on Fahey was no longer an option; with the way the block was, I was able to pull my car in front of his apartment. As soon as Fahey slipped the key into, the door lock, I fired. Hearing the shots, Fahey dove into the vestibule of his apartment.

"That night, Fahey went to Pudgie's house and told him, 'Gene just tried to kill me at my house.' Brian knew that was his only warning. From that point on, Fahey never missed a payment. Fahey was one of the most extreme cases where a deadbeat was being shot at or shot. Most of the time, the use of threats would get the point across. Telling a guy, 'Next time I'm gonna put my hands on you' was usually enough, and the threats escalated from there.

This was how the Mafia did things with the farmers and store keepers when they started in Sicily. A dead man could never pay.

Gene continued the story, "Dealing with Hintze and tending to Ronnie G's business was going smoothly. I would often stop by Ronnie's house to look in on Ronnie's kids to see how they were doing and to see if they needed anything. They ranged in age from twelve to twenty-one years old. Roe, the eldest at twenty-one, was a looker; we began dating, but it lasted only a short while. We were sneaking around so no one would know. I think since I was always around her house for years, we developed mutual curiosity about each other. Both of us did not want her father to find out, and we were both in relationships at the time. Had Ronnie found out, especially without me asking permission, there would have been hell to pay.

"My greatest concern was building up the loan money on the street to generate regular weekly income and to rebuild my sports book. Frank 'Bones' Caputo was in our crew; we would partner up and start a sports business. This time, instead of setting up a half-sheet with Ronnie G, I had a half-sheet with Bones. He had the bankroll if we ever got hit hard, but that was the exception. Between the sports book and vig, I could count on collecting five thousand a week at the low end. On a good week, nine, maybe ten, thousand. My business would steadily grow as time passed.

"Everything was going smoothly: my book and vig was ever increasing. I probably had a hundred thousand on the street for two points. My end, that was two grand a week I could rely on. Yeah, all my business was uneventful; those who borrowed from me knew my reputation for getting paid, so there were no games.

"While my business was running like a well-oiled machine, Pudgie was having a problem. Specifically, he was having a problem with this guy Luigi. He had borrowed forty-five thousand from Pudgie and was refusing to pay him. Pudgie had a conversation with Luigi, asking him for the payment. Luigi had told him he didn't have it and couldn't pay. Pudgie told him that was unacceptable. They went back and forth, and Luigi finally told Pudgie, 'Get it in blood.'

"Pudgie went to Hintze, telling him the forty-five thousand was Ronnie's money. Hintze explained everything to Ronnie when he visited him in prison. Ronnie gave Hintze his marching orders. When Hintze returned from the prison, he called me and told me to come over. We sat and talked, and he explained the entire situation to me. In my mind, I was second guessing his story. You see, Pudgie was neither feared nor respected. He was a money guy, a cash cow. The only reason he didn't get stiffed more frequently was because he was 'with' Ronnie G, and nothing more. For all I knew, the money was Pudgie's personal cash he had on the street or Luigi had owed him for drugs. Yes, even though he was not supposed to deal drugs, he did, big time. Ronnie G knew it as well, but turned a blind eye because Pudgie, his best earner, kept the cash flowing.

"Now I was being dragged into this bullshit. My past fights, beatings, and shootings had me being talked about as a 'cowboy.' My past willingness to exert Uncle Vin's and Ronnie's will made me their enforcer. I was fine with the role, but now I had to deal with this situation. Hintze had conveyed to me what Luigi had said, 'Get it in blood.' Using Luigi's own words against him, everything was set in motion. I would have to put a bullet into Luigi for Ronnie G to give him a warning.

"Luigi was from Howard Beach and I had known him for several years. When I got the order, I waited a couple of days, then headed over to his family's house. The house had too many security cameras to do anything. I had never actually formulated a plan to get him; actually, nothing ever came to mind.

"But I remember vividly how everything unfolded. It was mid-November, 2011, and the weather was tolerable. I had to meet a guy named Jared at Ragtime, a neighborhood grocery store that was frequented by everyone in the area. Jared had to give me a payment.

"We were sitting in my black Mercedes E-550 making small talk. I had asked him, 'Whatta ya doin now?'

"Jared replied, 'Oh, I gotta go meet Luigi.' "'What Luigi?' I asked. "It was him, but for the life of me, I cannot remember his last name. They were to meet at Park 207. Jared got out, and I immediately called Darren and gave him a coded message to get my gun and have it ready. I raced to his house in Lindenwood, a couple of minutes away, then over to Park 207. I gave Darren specific instructions: let me out on the corner of 88th Street and

160th Avenue. Looking up 88th Street, I could see Luigi's blacked out Hummer H2. It was him for sure. I told Darren go down to159th Avenue and wait for me.

"When I began walking towards Luigi's Hummer, the plan was further unfolding in my head. Ideally, I would walk up to the vehicle on the driver's side, open the door, and shoot Luigi in the leg. Should the door be locked, I would fire several rounds into the door in the area where Luigi's legs would be located. I got lucky. I was able to close the distance from where Darren had dropped me off to the vehicle without him noticing me. It was eleven o'clock at night, and I used the darkness and shadows to my advantage. The Hummer was right there. I grabbed the door handle with my left hand, yanked it open fast, and pressed the barrel of the nine-millimeter Hi-Point pistol to Luigi's left thigh. His quick and intentional reflexes surprised me.

He managed to grab my hand clenching the pistol before I could fire into his leg. He grabbed hold of my hand and attempted to divert the inevitable discharge, causing the gun to fire and hit him just above the groin area. He didn't know he was shot; the adrenaline was pumping for both of us. The tussle for the weapon angered me, and I pointed the pistol at his head and fired. Luigi instantly released my hand. The bullet had grazed his face. While all this was going on, Sean Cammarota was sitting in the passenger seat. He was in shock.

"At a flat run, I got to my vehicle within thirty seconds. Darren was behind the wheel, and I jumped in the passenger seat. I told Darren, 'Go!' Darren drove to my apartment and dropped me off, and he kept my car for a bit.

"I told him, 'Let me get cleaned up, I'll give you a call.' I stripped off the clothes I was wearing and threw them in the trash; later, I would dispose of the trash bag somewhere. Going into my kitchen, I grabbed a bottle of vinegar and washed my arms up to the elbow, hopefully to wash away any powder traces.

"Fifteen to twenty minutes passed, and I gave Darren a call; he was at my apartment within five minutes. Opening the driver's door, I told Darren, 'I'll drive.' Darren jumped out and went around the car. Behind the wheel, I drove back to the area; sure enough, yellow 'CRIME SCENE' tape and cops were all over. There was an ambulance, too. At that point, I did not know specifically what had occurred. I learned late that night or early morning that Luigi was shot above the groin and received a graze on his face. But my greater concern was Sean. I was on parole; if he gave my name to the law, I would be in prison for the next twenty years on a good day.

"A few days later, I went to Gold's gym to work out, and I bumped into Luigi's brother, Phil. He wanted to talk about what happened. I said to Phil, 'Everything alright?' implying there was a problem. Phil explained that Luigi was not going to give me up to the law. I told Phil, 'That's what happens when you tell people you're not gonna pay Ronnie.'

"Phil said, 'It's not what you think.' And I let it go, but I had a good idea what he meant. The debt was probably a personal debt that Pudgie turned into a loan debt by lying to Hintze. It had to be a loan debt in order to get me to collect 'Ronnie's money' for Pudgie.

"If it were a drug debt, neither I nor Ronnie could get involved. But Phil did let me know that detectives had gone to the hospital with my picture, insisting to Luigi that, 'this was the guy that shot you.' When I heard that, my mind started racing, trying to figure out who identified me. Had it been Luigi, the detectives would have arrested me immediately, so it was someone else. It had to be Sean Cammarota. I convinced myself this guy would cause me to go to prison for the next twenty years. In retrospect, his testimony alone was not enough; the District Attorney's Office would need a second witness to corroborate his testimony or other evidence. Let's face it, if the victim is saying it's not me, there is no case. My paranoia sent me down a dangerous path.

Convinced that Sean had told on me, and he probably did, I had to protect myself. After stewing for a couple of days, I had come up with a plot. I needed Darren to assist.

"Darren and I had become close as time went by. Initially he had owed me seven thousand dollars between loan money and sports money. I have to give him credit, he came to me, straight up and said, 'Gene, I can't pay, let me work it off.' I accepted. His physique was intimidating: two hundred and twenty pounds, five foot, eleven inches tall, and strong as a bull. He would become my partner on home invasions and armed robberies. He was basically a virgin to crime; he caught on fast and became good at it. I think he found his calling.

"We went to my social club when I decided to move forward with my scheme. I explained to Darren I wanted him to do two things and that I would pay him for each.

"First, I wanted him to help me dig a hole four feet deep, and I would pay him five hundred dollars. We would dig in an area known as 'the weeds' in Howard Beach. It was a completely desolate and remote area. Second, I wanted him to get Sean Cammarota and bring him to me at that location, and I would pay him five thousand dollars. Sean wasn't going to come willingly. Darren would have to take him by force --kidnap him. Darren didn't know Sean's habits, so I took him around Howard Beach and Middle Village to show him all the places Sean frequented. From that point on, Darren would be on his own. When he went out looking for Sean, he would contact me, and I would go to the road by the hole and wait. This would go on for about two weeks with absolutely no luck. Or maybe I was very lucky, for had Darren dropped off Sean and left, I would have killed him when he really was not a threat.

"The reason Darren could not find Sean over the course of those two weeks was because Sean fled to Las Vegas. He had gotten a job working at one of the casinos there; his fear saved his life.

"I received a message from the prison from Ronnie. It was extreme, but it was also my job as Ronnie's enforcer.

"Rachel Rosetti had no idea she would cause the contemplation of her father's murder. Vincent 'Vinny' Rosetti was one of Ronnie G's closest friends. But when the indictment would come down, Vinny would become an informant against Ronnie, forcing Ronnie to take a plea from the government. He would also provide information against Jerry Asaro and Jerry's cousin, Jackie, causing all of them to take a plea deal as well. The three guys were sore; nobody appreciated a rat in their midst. But in mob life, it came with the territory.

"Ronnie got a seven-and-a-half-year sentence.

"About four to five years into his sentence, Rachel Rosetti began coming up to Howard Beach from Florida. She was visiting because she wanted to see her friends.

"She had stayed in contact through social media but longed to go back home. She would travel back and stay with her closest friend, Brianna Ruggerio, whose father coincidently was a well-respected made guy with the Gambino crime family. Having a rat's daughter stay at the house while her father was serving time was a no-no. Rachel and Brianna were hanging out around the neighborhood, hitting the clubs, socializing, just enjoying themselves. The problem was that she was in the midst of the largest organized crime city in the United States ,and her every move was being seen and talked about. There are always prying eyes.

Social media puts every move you make on blast for the world to know. Seeing Rachel around was driving Ronnie's daughter, Roe, crazy. She was pissed. Rachel's dad, the rat, was living free in Florida, posting pictures with Rachel on Instagram, while Roe had to visit her dad in prison. During those visits, she let Ronnie know, and from what I was told by Hintze, she was relentless in her complaining. It took a hold on Ronnie and got him upset to the point he wanted to take action.

"During one of Ronnie's regular visits with Hintze, he

gave him instructions on what he wanted done: find out anything and everything you can on Vinny Rosetti. Hintze got on it, and I don't know how, but he had a trove of information -specific, too. Vinny was living and working as a real estate agent in Orlando. We had obtained his home and work address. His wife was with him as well. Ronnie was ready to make a move. The next time Hintze saw Ronnie, he was told to get Gene and say to him, 'I want you to take care of it.' Hintze conveyed the message and instructed me to take Pudgie.

"I said, 'No, I'll take one of my guys.' Somehow, Ronnie was communicating with Bonanno wiseguys from jail, but I'll never know how. Regardless, he was waiting for approval to come so he could have a federal witness killed.

"It just goes to show you, a guy's daughter starts crying to her daddy, and another guy is on the verge of dying. All it takes is getting the wrong person pissed off, and somebody dies. Once the order is given, it becomes a matter of time, for everything has been put in motion.

"Approval would never come. I assume Ronnie was seeking permission from his captain, Jerry Asaro. Even though Vinny Rosetti ratted on Jerry, he weighed the situation and denied Ronnie's request. The fallout from killing a federal witness would have been horrendous, the benefit negligible. The killing of a witness is a death penalty offense. Should anyone with knowledge of the murder cooperate with the feds, the government would have sought the death penalty of everyone involved. The shooter, I, and all the guys giving the orders would have their heads on the chopping block. Jerry made the right decision. One slip brings down the entire structure of a crew and possibly the entire criminal organization."

GENE RUNS RONNIE G'S BUSINESS

Gene Borrello goes on about his life with Vin Asaro and Ronnie G:

"When Uncle Vin's trial concluded in November, 2015, I was already in jail. I had been arrested in September, 2014, for gun sales, gun possession, and conspiracy.

"Watching television at Rikers Island, I was completely shocked at the verdict. But I am getting ahead of myself and must backtrack to April, 2013, when Ronnie G wrapped up his federal sentence and came home.

"Ronnie would be on federal supervised release, the equivalent of being on parole. While on supervised release, an ex-convict is not supposed to be around other ex-cons, but this rule is not strictly enforced. However, on federal supervised release, a made member, such as Ronnie G, cannot be seen with other members.

"The parole officer will be given a list by either the F.B.I. or the United States Attorney's Office of the known organized crime figures to ensure there is no meeting with Ronnie G.

"Ronnie didn't come directly home; the Federal Bureau of Prisons released him to a Community Corrections Center, or halfway house. Ronnie would have to find a job, which was not a problem, as one of his crew owned a deli. The deli sold bagels, coffee, groceries, had tables for patrons to relax and enjoy their purchases. Rob Pisani wasn't a known organized crime member.

In reality, he was a legitimate businessman who happened to be friends with Ronnie and occasionally dabbled in illegal enterprises. Pisani hired Ronnie, essentially giving him a no-show job.

"Ronnie did not have to do any work, and he was being paid four hundred dollars a week, but Ronnie was reimbursing Pisani. For the period Ronnie was there, we occupied a table at the back of the deli. The place became our center of operations, a social club to hang out and conduct business. Pisani's wife was not a happy camper. Since it was a public place, Mafiosos could come and go, bump into Ronnie, exchange pleasantries, make a purchase, and go about their business. Pisani's wife was witnessing the activities and could do nothing about it; she didn't like our kind. Not so much that we were gangsters, but we were violent gangsters.

"The deli would be our headquarters for four months, but the first month was the most intense. Ronnie's curfew from the halfway house was something like 7:00 a.m. to 5:00 p.m. I would pick Ronnie up and drop him off daily. As long as Rob Pisani claimed Ronnie was on the premises working or out running errands for the business, he was okay. Actually, Ronnie and I had become suspicious that no one ever called or came around to check on him. Parole Officers are usually very diligent when it came to known Mafia membership.

"Our daily routine together was me picking Ronnie up or meeting him at the deli; we would have breakfast and talk business. Around eleven or noon, we would hit the gym.

Ronnie was a workout guy, about five foot, nine inches, a little over two hundred pounds, stocky, and for a fourty-three-year-old guy, very strong. A genuine tough guy, Ronnie was a gangster, the real deal.

After the workout, back to the deli for lunch. Ronnie also was in the midst of building a home, new construction, from the ground up.

The house was at least six thousand square feet and probably closer to ten thousand. The place was huge. Part of our daily routine, actually a very large part of our routine, was picking up and lending money. Ronnie got the sports book up and running; I had to manage everything. We would have dinner every day at Ronnie's house with his family. Then back to the halfway house.

"Ronnie would be in the halfway house for one month, then they put him on a tether, or ankle bracelet. Ronnie and I, like before, were joined at the hip. We were always close, very close, to the point where the other guys in the crew were envious. There is one reason why I was treated more favorably than the others. In all respects, Ronnie always treated me as an equal. There is one reason for this. He was brought up and learned the life from Uncle Vin; the old man loved Ronnie because he was a gangster like himself, old school. Ronnie brought me up and taught me the life, as well as Uncle Vin, and Ronnie loved me for the same reasons. I conducted myself as Ronnie did, like an old-school gangster. Willing to fight, shoot, or kill. Because of this, we were in each-other's company every single day.

"Though Ronnie was done with the halfway house, he still

maintained the deli as his base of operations. We were in and out all day long. One thing we made time for every day was to play video games. Appreciate the irony: I'm twenty-nine, Ronnie is forty-three, we're both gangsters playing fuckin' video games. Both of us were sports guys, and we both loved football. Madden football was our game. After spending over seven years in prison, Ronnie and I would be sitting on the couch on the edge of our seats, rapidly pressing buttons to control the players. In retrospect, I think about the crazy shit we had done together, sitting there like two kids playing video games. Every so often, I would look at Ronnie and remember this guy was worth tens of millions of dollars and be in awe of his life.

"Ronnie, fresh out of prison, money readily available, wanted to shop. Every other day, we were out buying this or that, spending thousands. And you have to understand that Ronnie had to have the best, no matter what it was. We shopped everywhere, but Ronnie especially liked Bloomingdale's. It was nothing for Ronnie to slap down thirty grand for a watch for himself and one for his wife. While Ronnie was away, I had built up my loans and sports book money and had made a couple nice scores. Shopping together, I had no problem keeping pace with Ronnie's spending.

"We were together all day, every day. When the day would be winding down, Ronnie's wife, Tish, would set a plate for me at the dinner table. I ate with his three daughters, son, mother, and wife more than I had dinner with my own family. To me, Ronnie was my boss, older brother, and close friend. I cannot emphasize how close we always were, before and after his incarceration. Both of us being in the life brought our loyalty to one another to the next level.

"Few guys get to Ronnie's level; he was now on the fast track to becoming a captain. I tended to his business while he was away, protecting his empire. He could have used several other guys, but he relied on and trusted me. We were both earning big money, and neither of us had any problem spending to get what we wanted.

"A bonus to being over at Ronnie's house all the time was getting to see Uncle Vin. He would stop over to visit his sister and Ronnie, and the three of us would hang out. Once the three of us were alone, the Mafia talk would start. Vin, Ronnie, and I would talk about everything going on in the streets. Vin would keep us up to speed with anything at his level. Not only was I with them, they treated me as family.

Once talk of the Mafia started, Uncle Vin, with his high pitched voice, would start his ranting and raving.

"I loved when he was on a roll. Maintaining a serious face, I was breaking up on the inside. Vin would go on a tirade about this guy or that guy. He might take a breather and start up all over again. He would rant about his son, a Mafia captain, saying, 'Look at my son. He's got no balls.' Vin was truly the best and truly crazy. Psychopathic and a complete character. Ronnie and I would usually take care of Vin. If we were out shopping, we would pick him up something. Ronnie would always ask Uncle Vin, 'How you doin?'

"Vin would say, 'Not too good,' and Ronnie and I would give him some cash to hold him over. But it wouldn't matter; Vin was a compulsive gambler. If we gave him a million, he would be broke in the blink of an eye. Even the eight hundred thousand he had gotten from the Lufthansa Heist was gone in two months.

"Handing over five hundred or a thousand to Uncle Vin was no big deal. Ronnie's loan and sports book was growing and thriving. He was averaging fifty thousand, and I was averaging five to ten thousand a week. Money was never a problem; my problem was keeping some for a rainy day. Nope. I was on the gravy train and knew it would go on forever.

"We were sailing along, doing well, enjoying life and eachother's company when a more serious side of criminal life had to be addressed.

"It was around May, 2013, when a problem arose with one of Ronnie's crew members. Known as Simone, he was building his own loan shark business. Borrowing from Ronnie at one point and lending at three points. He had 220,000 dollars on the street at two points net. Simone should have been making forty-four hundred a week his end. Great money for very little work. While Ronnie was away, Simone was dealing with Hintze. He began having problems with the money. Nothing serious, but noticeable. Sometimes he would not pay; other times, he would be short and he would make it up. When Ronnie came home, Simone stayed on point with the money, paying Ronnie his end on time, every time.

"Pudgie and I had heard Simone had acquired a drug

problem. Word had it that he was using roxies,[11] crushing the pills and snorting the powder. The pills were only twenty-five dollars apiece; Simone should have been able to handle all his expenses and his habit.

"Not so. He started dipping into the loan money, reducing his weekly income, then got to a point where he couldn't keep up. Ronnie may have heard he was having problems, but he didn't believe it, and Simone kept his payments correct since Ronnie got home. And since he was one of our crew, Ronnie gave him the benefit of the doubt.

"Ronnie, Pudgie, and I were at the deli, and in comes Simone. Simone sat down told Ronnie, 'Ron I need thirty.'

"Ronnie replied, 'Stop by the house.' As soon as Simone left, Pudgie and I told Ronnie, 'Do not give him any more money. He's not the same guy.' Ronnie responded, 'Youse don't tell me what to do with my money, I know him twenty years.'

"One week passed, and I went to make my pickup from Simone. He was five hundred short. No surprise. I already knew where this was going. Been doing this too long not to, I cannot understand why Ronnie didn't see it or put faith in what we told him.

"The following day, I was at Ronnie's house in the morning, around ten o'clock, when Simone stopped by to pick up the money. From that moment, I watched Ronnie place three packs of ten thousand in Simone's hands I knew this was going to end badly.

---

[11] Roxicodone, a pain-reliever drug derived from morphine.

While Ronnie was away, Simone's nickname between me and Pud gie was 'The Junkie.' And you don't put thirty grand in the hands of a junkie.

Now I had to go back to Ronnie and tell him. This is a guy who questioned why a guy was short ten dollars; for five hundred, he would go ballistic. I might have dreaded telling Ronnie, but while driving, I had to call Pudgie to tell him. He picked up immediately, 'Pudge, I just met up with The Junkie, he shorted us five hundred.'

"Pudgie, in a slow, laid-back, raspy voice, said, "Whaaaat, this guy's gonna flip out!'

"It just so happened that when I spoke to Pudgie, we were both in transit to go to the deli to meet up with Ronnie. I think Pudgie was so anxious to see Ronnie's expression, he raced to the deli to ensure he was there before I arrived. Pudgie never liked Simone; I never knew why, but I sensed Pudgie knew this would be Simone's downfall.

"When I walked into the deli, I could see Pudgie sitting with Ronnie at a distance. It took every bit of self-control I had not to smirk; it got harder as I got closer to Ronnie. I reached the table, slid into the booth next to Pudgie, and told Ronnie, 'You're not gonna be happy about this.'

"Ronnie said, 'About what?'

"'Simone, he shorted us five hundred.' Ronnie maintained his composure; he was ready to explode, but he couldn't. The same with us. Pudgie and I couldn't explode with laughter. We knew Ronnie for years; for him not to fly off the handle was abnormal. Ronnie, in a calm, measured voice, told me, 'If he's short again, bring 'em with ya.'

"The following week, I was making my pickups. I stopped over at Simone's house to collect his weekly payment. He was supposed to pay twenty-five hundred a week. Last week, he was short five hundred; this week, he was short one thousand. Ronnie would have a fit. I told Simone, 'Come on, you gotta come by the deli.' Simon got in; once he was settled in, I tried to have a conversation with him to figure out what was going on in his life and possibly come up with an answer. I tried to explain to Simone, telling him, 'Look, you got a quarter million on the street, you should not be short. You're upside down, are you jammed up?'

"Simone simply said, 'No.'

"I said, 'Listen. Simone, you know what I do, so tell me the truth.'

"Simone said, 'Nah, Gene, I'm okay.'

"I answered with reluctance, 'Okay, but you're gonna talk to this man.'

"Simone's demeanor was upbeat; this guy had no idea how much trouble he was in. He believed that because he knew Ronnie for twenty years, it wasn't a big issue. Simone did know Ronnie for twenty years, and he was in our crew, but the guy was delusional. The reality is, Simone was a worker. He put Ronnie's money on the street, made two points for himself and a point for Ronnie. Over time, Simone's loan book was up to a quarter million. Seventy-five hundred in collections a week: five thousand for Simone and twenty-five hundred for Ronnie. All Simone had to do was lend the money and pick up the weekly payments. If there was a situation he couldn't handle, should someone not want to pay, he could go to Ronnie, and Ronnie would have sent me to resolve the situation.

"That's what I did -I was muscle in Ronnie's crew, amongst other things. In Howard Beach, Simone should never have had a problem, for we ran the area. To stiff Ronnie would have been insane.

"While I was in the car with Simone, my phone rang. It was a text message from Ronnie: 'What's goin' on with him?' I texted back, 'No good. I'm bringing him over right now.' I know Ronnie; he's been lending money for twenty-five years, and he already knows Simone's situation. The sad part is that Simone had no clue that he was fucked. Ronnie knew where this was going, and he was getting himself all worked up. Taking Simone to the deli to meet with Ronnie was taking a lamb to the slaughter. I arrived at the deli and pulled into the rear parking area for the owners and employees. Simone and I exited the car and headed in. Ronnie was standing by our booth, waiting. His body language was not good. Simone still didn't have a clue. We approached Ronnie.

He said, 'Come on let's go outside.' Not good. The three of us exited the deli and were in the employees parking lot. It was fairly secluded. Ronnie immediately started in on him, 'Simone, what's goin' on, why you short two weeks in a row, are you jammed up?'

"Simone said in a cocky tone, 'Nah, what's the big deal?' Simone never saw it coming. Ronnie slapped him so hard that he knocked Simone to the ground. Once down, we both punched him and kicked him. Ronnie, a mere four or five weeks out of prison, still reporting back to the halfway house, was giving a guy a beating. He was paranoid and realized passerby may see what was going on. My truck was right there. Ronnie said, 'Put him in the truck, put him in the truck.' We lifted Simone to his feet and put him on the passenger seat. Ronnie got in the back seat, and I got in the driver side.

"Ronnie was screaming at Simone, 'Where's the money, wha'd you do with it?' Simone didn't answer.

"Ronnie hollered louder than I thought possible, 'What ya do with the thirty grand I just gave you?'

"Simone answered, 'I used it for the house.' Simone was terrified; he thought we were going to kill him. Once he told Ronnie he used the money for the house, we started beating him again. Ronnie was throwing punches from the back seat. Having brass knuckles in the door compartment, in the midst of the action, I slipped them on my right hand and began giving Simone backhands. The first swing caught Simone on the forehead.

He brought his arms immediately up to cover his face. With the brass knuckles in the mix, he didn't seem to mind Ronnie's punches. I never punched him with the weapon. I hit him with backhands and an open hand, but that metal hurts. I watched many a guy wince in pain; Simone was no different -he winced, moaned, and balled himself up as tightly as humanly possible. The beating ceased. Ronnie was still worked up; of all of us, his adrenaline was pumping the most. There was a moment of calm, and I noticed a horrid smell. I said to Ronnie, 'I think he shit himself.' He did.

"Ronnie now still angry started barking orders at me, 'Do not let him outta your sight. Get Pudgie and go to his house and get my fuckin' list.' Without missing a beat, he turned to Simone and told him, 'And you, you piece of shit, I know you twenty years, and you do this to me.' With that, Ronnie got out of the truck and went into the deli, leaving me and Simone in the truck.

"I turned to Simone and, with a raised voice, said, 'What's wrong with you? I told ya this was goin' to happen.'

"Simone responded, 'I can't believe Ronnie did this to me. I know the guy twenty years.'

"Pudgie is usually in the area; once Ronnie called, he was there in fifteen minutes. He pulled into the employee lot, saw my truck, and pulled up. I had gotten out, approached his car, and told him, 'Park, we're using my car.' I explained what happened and what we had to do. Ronnie and I had taken Simone's phone. Pudgie went through the guy's phone to see if there were any names he recognized or if there was any other information that might be relevant.

"I pulled away and headed to Simone's house. It was only ten minutes away. Parked in front of his house, Simone tried to get out of the truck without us. I told him, 'Hold up, wait for us, we're coming.'

"The three of us entered Simone's house; his wife happened to be home. When she laid eyes on her husband, she knew something was very wrong, knew Ronnie, and was terrified. Rightfully so. We go into the kitchen, and the three of us sit down. His wife went into another room to wait.

"The list tells us everything. How much is lent, to whom, at what rate, and contact information. Once we get the list, we can figure out exactly what the prick was doing or not doing with Ronnie's money.

"Sitting at the table, I told Simone, 'Go get the list.' And he doesn't want to; after all he's been through, he's given us the runaround. I told him a few more times, 'Go get the fuckin' list.' He persisted. I had to actually beat the guy up some more, and he would not relent. When I told him I was going to stab him, he finally went and got the list. We let him go unescorted. He went to his bedroom and returned with the debt list.

"Once we had the list in hand, we went back to the deli. We gave Ronnie the list; he poured over it and realized Simone was collecting twenty-six hundred in vig per week. Had he put all of it on the street, he would have been collecting seventy-five hundred total per week. Simone fucked up. Drug dealers aren't supposed to use their own product, and loan sharks aren't supposed to use their own supply. Simone had been spending Ronnie's money instead of lending it. I imagine this happened over a long period of time. When Ronnie tallied everything up, Simone had approximately one hundred thousand on the street; the other hundred and fifty grand was missing.

"When Ronnie realized how much was missing, he was furious, and that's being kind. There was only one way Ronnie saw this: the guy robbed him for a hundred and fifty grand, and Ronnie was going to get it back somehow.

If not in cash, then in blood. Before you know it, word would spread, and Ronnie would be looked at as a soft touch. It wasn't happening. For a quarter million dollars, guys would be lining up to take a beatin'.

"When Ronnie finally calmed down, and it took a while, he had sent me and Pudgie back to Simone's house the same day. I knocked, and Simone's wife answered the door. Both of us were standing there. I told the wife, 'Go get Simone.'

"She said no and shut the door. Simone knew at that point that Ronnie figured out he blew a hundred and fifty thousand and assumed we were going to kill him.

"For the next week, I would go over his house, and no

one would bother to answer the door. Ronnie would have me lay on the house to try to catch him, should he come out.

"One day, I get a call from John 'Bazoo' Ragano, a Bonanno family member. He called regarding the situation with Simone. Simone's brother-in-law, Kenny, was put on record by Ragano, and Kenny had gone to Ragano to get him to intervene.

Kenny's name was on the deed of Simone's house; they were partners. I explained to John how serious it was. He said, 'Don't worry about that, we're working on something to straighten everything out. Tell Ronnie I'll give you a call in a couple of days to arrange a meeting.' Three days later, I got a call from Bazoo. He told me, 'I'm gonna come by now, is it okay?'

"I said, 'Yeah.' Ronnie, standing next to me, said, 'Tell him to go around back.' I conveyed the message. Bazoo arrived about twenty minutes later with Kenny and Simone in the car. He parked in the employee lot. The three guys came into the back of the deli. Several guys sat in the booth, and a couple of chairs were pulled up to the table. Pudgie was there with us.

Kenny began to speak, explaining the plan they had to recoup Ronnie's hundred and fifty grand. It was simple and straight forward: the three-family house would be sold. The house was valued at eight hundred thousand and was nearly paid off. Once the house was sold, none, not one penny of the money, would be put in the hands of Simone. As soon as the house was sold, Ronnie's money would be taken off the top, and Ronnie would be paid. The mere presence of Bazoo, a wiseguy, was vouching that Kenny would do the right thing. Ronnie agreed to Kenny's proposal and made one last statement before the meeting convened. Ronnie said it in front of everyone very matter-of-factly: 'You're giving me your word I will be paid. If I'm not, I'm giving you my word: we're gonna kill him.'"

RUSTY MONEY

Borrello continued the story of Simone:

"The presence of Bazoo vouching for Simone made all the difference. When the meeting concluded and the three guys left, Ronnie told me, 'Don't bother him no more. If he doesn't pay, he's fuckin' dead.'

"Simone was in a no-win situation, and there were only the two choices: pay or die. Even though he had a made guy to speak for him, mob politics were completely against Simone. If he were to deviate in any way, he would have gotten a beating or killed. The intervention of Bazoo on Simone's behalf simply guaranteed his safety until the debt was paid. Had the debt not been paid, Simone's brother-in-law, Kenny, and Bazoo would have had to serve him up to be killed. Even more so because they were all Bonanno guys. Had a made guy from another family intervened, the outcome would have been the same. It wasn't a situation that could have been squashed.

"The house would finally be sold in February, 2014. It took several months, but Ronnie got paid. Ronnie was even getting paid the vig from Simone's list and a little extra. Simone's weekly payments were supposed to be twenty-five hundred. Since Ronnie was now collecting three points, he was actually being paid twenty-six hundred a week from Simone's list. I always said this guy falls ass-backwards into money.

"Not only was Ronnie collecting an extra C-note, he wound up putting out another hundred thousand with the guys from Simone's list. I was taking care of all this for

Ronnie, and I saw the client list grow.

"Before we settled the Simone affair around July, 2013, Ronnie was still on supervised release, but he was settling in and getting comfortable. While he was away, several of his crew had set up sports books.

"Associates can set up their own sports books, but they have to kick up an envelope to their boss. There are few independents, simply because they don't have enough cash to take big bets. Ronnie would let a guy bet fifty thousand a game. His sports book was so big, he was doing half-sheets with other Mafia families.

Ronnie simply had a pile of cash on hand, and he made every dollar work for him in the most reliable ways he knew: shylocking and sports action. In sports, the payoffs were great, but Ronnie, as the bank, took all the risk.

"Now that Ronnie was settled in, all his guys that were doing sports had to use him as the bank and set up half-sheets with Ronnie.

"Joe DiCarrio, a hang-around guy, did sports, loan sharking, and would find scores, then hand them off. On the scores, Joe would get an equal share, usually one third. He was doing things with the Genovese guys but was not put on record. Eventually, he took a pinch with some Genovese guys and went to federal prison in Fort Dix, New Jersey. At Fort Dix, he had met Ronnie. Joe wasn't a made member, but he was around the mob and knew how to act and talk around mob guys. Ronnie took a liking to Joe. When you do time with a guy and keep each other's company and watch each other's back, it is a genuine bonding experience. Joe had gotten out three years before Ronnie. Ronnie had told Joe to go see Hintze and me, and we would get him started. Joe put Ronnie's money on the street, same deal as everyone else. Joe got the money at one point and lent it at three points. As far as we could see, he was making money. Then one day, he disappears for a month. Nothing, no phone calls, never answered, and never stopped around.

"Hintze went to see Ronnie, told him about Joe. Ronnie being Ronnie had one answer, 'Send Gene.' He told me, 'Don't shoot him, just scare him, pistol whip him.' Once I got word, I started calling Joe and telling him, 'I'm gonna be outside your house.' After one of the unanswered calls, Joe unexpectedly called back.

"I said to him, 'Joe, I gotta come see ya.'

"Joe said in a meek and surprised voice, 'You gonna shoot me?'

"I replied, 'I'm on my way.'

"Until I got word from Hintze, I remained in transit. Hintze called in a couple of minutes and told me, 'He's gonna meet me, so go back.' I pulled a U-ey and headed home. The fact that I was headed there to see Joe about his missing payments was enough to get him back on track. He paid four weeks back for his vig and made all his remaining payments. Guys in the street knew I was Ronnie's muscle. If you're short and I'm coming to see you, you're probably going to get pistol whipped.

"When Ronnie came home, Joe expanded his business by setting up a half-sheet with Ronnie to take sports action.

Joe had us believing he was expanding his business; that was all bullshit. Joe had one customer -Joe. He set up the half-sheet for himself. This way, if he lost fifty grand, he would have to pay Ronnie twenty-five. And Joe wasn't betting games; all his bets were on horses. He had ten accounts with a maximum bet per account at five thousand dollars. Joe was banging out fifty thousand in losses a week, week in and week out. Ronnie knew what he was doing, and there was nothing wrong with it, just as long as Ronnie got his fifty percent of the betting activity.

"Rusty money, no. It's not a nickname of a wiseguy, it's what was driving me and Ronnie crazy. Like I said, Joe was losing weekly. Because he had a half-sheet with Ronnie, I did all the pickups. Every week, the same thing, he paid us with rusty money. Ronnie and I were joking about this money. It really was not 'rusty money,' it was water-damaged, and the dates on the bills were always 1999 or 2000. All totaled, Joe probably paid Ronnie a quarter million dollars over a period of four months. Joe was a compulsive gambler; there was no stopping him. The only way guys like Joe stopped, if they ever stopped, was to hit rock bottom.

"The whole time he was paying us with rusty money, Ronnie and I may have been laughing about it, but I was pissed off. What Ronnie didn't know was that I was doing scores for Joe. He had access to inside information on scores, and I did armed robberies on the side. I also had a couple of guys with me who were ready to go at any time. My deal with Joe was an equal share for everyone. Three guys, thirty-three percent apiece.

"Howard Beach and the surrounding areas are very

provincial, and being involved in organized crime, you hear everything about everybody. I started hearing Joe was spending money all over the area: forty thousand for an engagement ring, paid Ronnie 120,000 dollars in rusty money, fifty thousand to Bonanno gangsters, and more. With all the money he had already lost to Ronnie and his spending, his gambling was not slowing down. The guy had to have pulled down a million-dollar score.

"And he passed me up on the big score, but on the three jewelry stores, two went bad. My friend, Darren, got pinched and was serving five years. On top of everything, when he paid off a debt in Middle Village, Joe bragged, 'I got the big one, finally.' Once I heard that, the next time I saw Joe that Wednesday, to pick up the sports money, I mentioned it to him.

"I explained to him, 'Listen, Joe, I heard from a guy in Middle Village that you did a big score. You know I do the scores; you give me the crazy cowboy jobs and then leave me out of the big one. That's fucked up. I got a guy doin' five years from the one jewelry store.'

"Joe said, 'Gene, it was a spur-of-the-moment thing. I did it myself.' I was sore with him for not including me, but the animosity passed.

"The following Wednesday when I went to see Joe to pick up the sports money, e hands me thirty grand. I asked, 'What's this for?'

"Joe replied, 'I thought about what you said last week, and I was wrong, I shoulda called ya.'

"I appreciated Joe's candor and generosity; he didn't have

to give me a dime. Darren was serving five years. I would give him money through his father and sister. When Joe gave me the thirty grand, I gave Darren's father five thousand for Darren.

"While Ronnie was serving time in Fort Dix, New Jersey, he befriended Joey Amato, a skipper with the Colombo Family out of Brooklyn.

"When Amato was released from prison, Ronnie gave him 150,000 dollars to put on the street at a two percent vig back to Ronnie. Well, Amato disappeared without any weekly payments.

"Ronnie was furious when he got out of jail in 2010. Mike Hinsey was supposed to collect the money from Amato, but he couldn't. Ronnie gives Hinsey the order to get Amato. The problem is, Amato couldn't be touched because he's a skipper. Hinsey, the nervous type, wanted to go after Amato. I told him we would both get a bullet in the head if we did anything.

"I had to figure out a way to get Amato's attention. I knew there was this guy who was a plumber and did shy for Amato. I went to the plumber and abused him verbally. Then I choked him a bit and I pulled a pistol on him and threatened that he would be hurt if we didn't get the money. The guy was petrified, and of course, he ran to Amato.

"Amato and Ronnie had a sit-down and settled the matter for 1,000 dollars a week. Case closed. The story would have had a bloody ending if we followed Ronnie G's orders."

RONNIE G AND THE GAMBINOS

For nearly fifteen years, there had been bad blood between Ronnie G and the Gambino crime family. Ronnie had an entire Mafia family angry with him. Amongst Italians, vengeance runs deep. A lot of people didn't care for Ronnie G's personality and habits, which contributed to the immense dislike toward him. The Gambinos and members of his own crew disliked him to the point of hatred.

Borrello remained loyal...at least for a while.

"To many people, Ronnie was an asshole. But he was our asshole.

"He was my direct boss, make no mistake. I would do anything for him, and there would come a time when we would have a serious falling out. As bad as he could be, sometimes he was right. When a gangster is right and mob rules come into play, even with the politics, at the end of the day, right is right and wrong is wrong.

"A Gambino guy was dating Ronnie's niece, Anita.

"She was seeing a guy named Nicky Corozzo -his entire family was Mafioso. His father was a made guy, one uncle was the consigliere, and another uncle was an underboss.

"The Gambino family is deep with Corozzo's. Anita's family is Uncle Ronnie, a made member, Jerry Asaro, Uncle Vin, and so much more. This couple's familial ties to organized crime runs deep and involves the hierarchies of both the Gambinos and the Bonannos.

"Ronnie had an especial affinity for Anita; he had taken her and her brother in to live with him when they were young. Having these kids in his household, Ronnie became their provider and absentee father. Years later, while in her twenties, Anita began dating Nicky. They were a young couple in love: passionate and hot headed, as Italians could be. During several arguments, Nicky had struck Anita. Like most domestic arguments, when the man hits the woman, he begs forgiveness and tells her, 'Baby, I love you, it'll never happen again.' But it recurs again and again, becoming a repetitive cycle. And finally, there's that one fight when the boyfriend goes too far. One night, she came home to Ronnie's house and was balling to him. Ronnie could see his beautiful niece beat up, physically abused by this piece of shit. Ronnie saw blood. Beating up a woman is a big no-no in mob life. It's predatory and cowardly.

"Ronnie took Padavona with him looking for Nicky Corozzo. They weren't going to kill him, but they planned on beating him with pipes. Driving in the car, they spotted Nicky, but Nicky saw them coming and ran. Nicky was too fast and managed to get away. Ronnie and Mike couldn't catch him; he was gone.

"Nicky knew his problem was at a whole other level. He went to his uncle's, the underboss, and consigliere to protect him. These Gambino guys reached out to Ronnie to have a sitdown.

"Ronnie agreed, but in reality, he had no choice but to go. He brought with him his captain, Jerry Asaro, and Uncle Vin. From what I know, it didn't go well. Ronnie wanted the Gambinos to serve up Nicky Corozzo to receive a beatin'. They said no. Ronnie made it clear to them he was gonna get Nicky. Nicky's uncles let him know he had a problem and that they couldn't protect him.

"Their only choice was to send him to Florida. "Nicky left for Florida, on the lamb from Ronnie G.

"One night, while living the good life down south, Nicky got jumped in a night club by several Rastafarians. They held him on the floor and cut his face with a broken bottle. The way everything unfolded and the severity of the cut was not from some problem in the club. After it happened, Ronnie would tell us he had it done. And knowing Ronnie, I can tell you, he doesn't lie about something like that or take credit for something he didn't do.

"A couple of years later, Nicky and I had a dispute over money. Arguing in Centerville Park in Ozone Park, Queens, Nicky took a swing at me and connected. He didn't faze me, and I went at him full bore, beating him badly. Luckily, one of his friends was there to pull me off and stop the fight. Later that day, when I went over Ronnie's house, he saw me at a distance, and I noticed he had a big smile on his face. Regarding the fight, Ronnie would always say, 'Another win for us.'

"To Nicky's credit, he came back two weeks later with his brother, and they were trying to beat me with baseball bats. I never got hit, and my guys intervened to stop it from going further. Being who they were, it was unacceptable for them to lose a fight and an embarrassment to their very connected family. To add insult to injury, in 2011, Blaze Corozzo and I were at an engagement party of a mutual friend, and he started an argument with me over some bullshit and punched me in the mouth. I unloaded a hard-right cross, and he was out. Fight over."

The beefs with the Gambinos seemed to come out of thin air. Al Trucchio, a skipper in the Gambino family, had a problem with Mike Palmaccio getting straightened out by the Bonannos.

Al's feeling was that Mike simply wasn't a gangster, not cut from the same cloth as Ronnie G and Uncle Vin, and believed he bought his button. Mike and Al had to meet for some reason. Al got in Mike's car and verbally abused him. Al pointed a gun to Mike's chest, insulting him further.

Borrello explains what happened next, "While Ronnie and Al were friends, had mutual respect, when Mike told Ronnie what Al did, he went off. Ronnie jumped in his car and called Al, telling him, 'I gotta see ya.' He went to see Al, slammed the shifter into park, got out of the car, and started in on Al, telling him, 'This bullshit's gotta stop with Mike.' "Al replied, 'Ron, I love you, respect you, but he's a jerk-off.' "Ronnie blurted out, 'You gotta respect him. He's a friend, and he's with me.'"

This saga would continue; this time, Palmaccio caused the problem by beating up a seventeen-year-old kid in a bagel store. As it turned out, the kid's uncle was a made guy in, of course, the Gambino family. Trucchio got wind of it and took advantage of the opportunity. Trucchio, with three other guys in the car, went searching for Mike. In the early morning, Trucchio and his car load of thugs forced Mike off the road. They dragged him out of the car and verbally and physically abused him, slapping Palmaccio and punching him around.

Borrello explains what happened next in detail:

"At the end of the day, Mike is a friend. Right after it happened, Mike called Ronnie and went over his house to tell him what happened. I don't know if Ronnie hollered at Mike, but I know Uncle Vin did, and when Uncle Vin starts screaming at you, calling you every insult imaginable, you know it and feel embarrassed. Vin was the best at it .

"Uncle Vin was the most upset because what happened to Mike would be all over the street and would be an embarrassment to the family. The next day, Ronnie called for all of his crew to explain the situation. To make things worse, Uncle Vin ordered retribution. Ronnie was hollering so loudly, his face was beet red. I thought we were going to kill someone. When Ronnie would get like this, people went silent, afraid to say the wrong thing. Ronnie said, 'We're goin' after 'Vinny Carwash.' I know where he lives.'

"I asked Ronnie, 'You want us to get 'em?'

"Ronnie replied, 'No, me and the fuckin' jerk-off, we'll go. You two watch from the corner.' Palmaccio wasn't there yet.

"That night, Ronnie G and Palmaccio were waiting by Vinny Carwash's house for him to close up his social club and head home. Bobby G and I were parked a short distance away watching; we were armed, should anything go wrong. From our vantage point, we watched the incident unfold.

"Vinny Carwash pulled up and parked his Dodge Ram truck, got out, and saw Ronnie and Mike Palmaccio coming at him.

Before he could react, Ronnie hit him with a slap-jack. Ronnie and Mike pummeled him, hitting him repeatedly, and left him in a pool of his own blood, gashes on his head. Vinny was badly beaten, to say the least."

The gamesmanship between the two families would be ongoing. Retribution for the Vinny Carwash beating was months away. Ronnie was on bail when the Vinny Carwash incident occurred. Al Trucchio would wait until Ronnie went to jail. Joey Scopo and Tony Muscatello called Mike Padavona and offered some ruse to go see him.

Borrello recalls, "They go meet Mike at his boathouse. Without warning, when they get close enough to Mike, they throw him into the water and say, 'Tell Ronnie what's up.' Even in prison, Ronnie would be told about the incident when he would get his update from Hintze."

Karma was not on Joey Scopo's side. A couple of years later, he would have to serve time for stealing Bobcats from construction sites. He had to serve his time at Fort Dix, New Jersey, the same place Ronnie G was serving his time.

Borrello picks up the story:

"Ronnie could be a prick; he was fearless, and he had

a long memory. When Joey hit the compound, Ronnie verbally abused him to the point where Joey wouldn't come out of his cell. The abuse was so bad, we heard about it on the street. When you send a message to a real tough guy, you better be prepared to back it up.

"While Ronnie was serving a seven-and-a-half-year sentence, he would come across another Gambino guy, 'Frankie Carwash.' They would hang out, play cards, and one day, Frankie got up from the card table, feigned being upset, and went to the bathroom. Ronnie went to check on him, asking, 'What's goin' on?'

"Frankie responded, 'It's nothin', I'm okay.'

"And it was done. They resumed their friendship, it was all good. Frankie went home. Three years after Frankie went home, Ronnie is released. When Ronnie gets home, he hears the story of how Frankie Carwash put Ronnie G in line in the bathroom. Ronnie was fuming. In prison, guys do this bullshit all the time: they pick a genuine tough guy, have a private conversation, and then walk away and tell a story how they 'checked' the guy.

"It's a dangerous game. And sometimes, the check comes due. Ronnie came home, and when he got out of the halfway house, he tricked Frankie into a meeting. Without warning, Ronnie knocked Frankie out, one and done. Right after, he called me on the phone and screamed into the phone, 'One shot, one shot, I knocked him out.' Frankie happened to be close friends with Bazoo, a Bonanno soldier, and he reached out to him. Bazoo came to Ronnie's house and told me he wanted to meet with me. Ronnie told John (Bazoo), 'Meet with him, see what he wants, I'm sending Gene and Chris, just in case.' Ronnie told me and Chris, 'If you see anyone come up on John, anything that looks suspicious, you start shooting.' John and Frankie were to meet at Ragtime, a general store in Howard Beach.

"Frankie had armed guys with him as well. At their meeting, nobody got shot or killed. Frankie Carwash said, 'It's not over.'

"When John conveyed Frankie's words to Ronnie' he said, 'He declared open season on himself.' Ronnie, whenever he would see Frankie, would abuse him in any way that he could. It got so bad, the Gambinos gave Frankie a button just to get Ronnie to stop.

"Ronnie and I were rocking and rolling. Money was pouring in from every angle. On the side, I was putting down scores, dabbling in drugs, and any other moneymaking opportunity that dropped at my feet. I was up for anything. All this criminal activity was off the books. I was not letting Ronnie know anything.

"Especially the drugs. Ronnie, as a gangster, was obligated to order me to stay away from drugs. And Ronnie, as always, fell ass-backwards into money, coming in hand over fist.

"Rob Pisani had put money on the street from Ronnie. Rob was a legitimate businessman, owned and operated several businesses. He had several delis, a bar and grill, residential rental properties, and store front rentals. The money he was putting on the street was to garner a little extra income. Rob had a quarter million on the street. I don't know exactly what happened, but Rob had gotten in trouble. Evidently, he lent a big chunk of the cash to someone who went bad on him, leaving Rob owning Ronnie a quarter million dollars. By now, I think it's abundantly clear, Ronnie is getting paid.

"Rob got in this trouble while Ronnie was in prison. Hintze visited Ronnie regularly and explained everything. Shortly thereafter, when Hintze saw Ronnie again, Ronnie told Hintze to go see Rob to make a deal for the money. Rob had a nice corner property in Howard Beach, and Ronnie wanted it to raze the house and build new. The property was valued at one million dollars. Ronnie offered eight hundred thousand for the house, forgave Rob all his debts, and Rob could continue to live on the property until Ronnie was released from prison. Rob would still have to pay the taxes and bills. Rob agreed to the deal. I don't know how, but I'm pretty sure Ronnie had pressed Rob in some way to do the deal.

When Ronnie came home, Rob moved out and had already bought a plot in Broad Channel, and he would break ground and build himself a house. It was around October, 2013, and construction was underway on both properties. Being on sight gave Ronnie something to do with his down time, which was bad for the laborers and the general contractor. Ronnie watched every fucking nail being hammered and every board being cut, and he wanted everything done a certain way. Ronnie was a job control freak, and he drove the workers crazy.

"Rob Pisani was Ronnie's childhood friend; he gave Ronnie a job at his deli to get him out of the halfway house. Ronnie, the greedy fuck that he was, knew Rob's property was under construction. Rob either told Ronnie what was going on or Ronnie visited Rob at the job site and found out there was twenty thousand in copper on the site. Ronnie sees me at his job site later that day and tells me what to do. Ronnie tells me to go over to Rob Pisani's construction site that night and steal all the copper. When it came to money, nothing that Ronnie would do would surprise me. Anyway, that night, I got my cousin to help me lug a large spool of copper. Once at the truck, it took us half an hour to get the damn thing loaded. I have no idea if Ronnie used the copper on his own house or if he sold it. I could go on with story after story; I cannot emphasize enough how greedy Ronnie was and the lengths he would go to for some extra cash. What adds insult to injury is the simple fact that Ronnie had five million in cash readily available."

Gene Borrello's value to Ronnie G was enormous, yet Gene's career in the mob was being hindered by his boss. Ronnie G's empire was growing rapidly, and Borrello was working literally seven days a week as an on-call enforcer. Borrello had to be ready at any time to either run a simple errand or bury a body.

Borrello knew the violence he carried out, although not on a daily basis, would strengthen his reputation in the Bonanno family and the Mafia in general. Gene kept the empire running and growing while Ronnie was away, which made his value indispensable.

Ronnie G told Vin Asaro just before he went to prison that Borrello 'was ready' to get his button.

Borrello explains, "For me to become a member, Ronnie

would have to be the one to, 'put me up,' no one else. I was his guy; it was his responsibility. He could have handed that responsibility off, but it was something he wanted to do himself. I believe Ronnie wanted to 'put me up' personally because he knew those like me were the next generation of the Mafia."

These days, the F.B.I.'s intelligence and informant network is so pervasive in Howard Beach, they would have known the following day that Borrello was made. New York and the Five Burroughs has the greatest concentration of Mafioso in America.

It has been that way since the 1920s and 1930s. Having that concentration of Mafioso has enabled the F.B.I. to modify and perfect their investigative techniques. Usually, each crime family: Colombo, Lucchese, Gambino, Genovese, and Bonanno, each had their own F.B.I. squad assigned to investigate and prosecute organized crime membership.

The F.B.I. knows a man's entire criminal career. Often, they can arrest someone, but they let him go on and on, and then when he gets around someone they want...they pounce.

When a prisoner is in lock-up, either at the precinct or Rikers Island, an Assistant United States Attorney and a couple of F.B.I. agents will make a friendly visit. The conversation begins with the individual's current arrest, and the agents will build from there. During an entire criminal career, once someone popped on their radar, they began watching closely. Photos, phone taps,information from credible witnesses, and credible informants, and now the individual is not just being charged with assault and battery, but with a plethora of other, more serious crimes.

Borrello speaks from first-hand experience:

"The A.U.S.A. will tell you, 'We have you dead to rights on the assault and battery. You are facing eight years. But when we file a superseding indictment, there will be two attempted murders, arson, robbery, home invasion, conspiracy. You will be facing thirty to life. You'll be home when you're sixty-five.'

"They will show the evidence, tell you who around you was wearing a wire or was a CI and now a cooperating witness. Cornered, no way out, your life is over; the next time you see the streets, decades will have passed. Guys can say whatever they want, but they're in your head, and you're thinking about everything they are saying. Deep down, you know they're not bullshitting; this is real, as real as anything can get.

"Then the A.U.S.A. will drop the bomb...'Or you can cooperate. Debrief. The United States Attorney's Office will file a letter or motion with the judge, and you will receive a significantly reduced sentence.'

"Yep, they got it down to a science.

"It's odd how paths cross in life and situations that are well in the past arise in the present. It was probably 2000, and a woman named Lisa, a civilian, was marked to die by Joe Massino, the Bonanno family boss.

"Joe was not a pushover or an easygoing boss. He ordered countless people murdered and had no problem doing his own work. Joe would readily pull the trigger. Lisa, even as a civilian, had crossed a line; she was a person who tended to push things to the limit, and this time, she went too far with the wrong person. Joe went so far as to order Lisa killed. Not only did he want her killed, he wanted it done in a very specific way. Joe was going to have one of his guys beat her to death with a pipe in front of her house.

"Someone, somehow, appealed to Joe's sensibilities, Lisa was granted a reprieve, but there would still be punishment. Lisa's truck was set on fire, totaled. Then, for some reason, Joe's guys grabbed Lisa's husband, threw him in the trunk, took him for a rough ride, and scared him to death. The poor guy didn't have a clue why mobsters were after him."

THINGS BEGIN TO CHANGE

The winds of change began to circle around Gene Borrello. He was beginning to see the hypocrisy and treachery in the life. Although not an educated person, not book smart, Borrello was street smart and savvy in his own right. He was not a great reader, but he had almost a photographic memory for things he sees and hears.

Here, he tells the story about his beginning to come out of the great abyss of the Mafia life:

"It was April, 2012. I was out sporting around in a BMW 750i with my friend, Lawrence. The car was a month old, and I just loved driving it. It was the nicest car I ever had. Driving to Ragtime, a local deli and hangout, I see an attractive blonde at a distance go into the store and say to Lawrence, 'Who the fuck is that?'

"'I don't know,' he replied.

"In our area, I know most everybody, but this girl was a stranger. While I was at the light, I see the blonde come out, and she happened to get into an Acura.

"It was my cousin's car. I pulled over and walked to her car to say hello. I introduce myself to the blonde, 'Hey I've never seen you around here before, and I know all the hot women in Howard Beach.'

"'I'm Samantha, and I've lived here my whole life.' "'You have a boyfriend?'

"Samantha replied, 'Yes.'

"'Alright, you won't have one for long.'

"Samantha laughed, and I said, 'I'll see you around.'

"I turned my attention to my cousin and told her, 'Justine, I'll text you later.' I texted her immediately and told her, 'Hook me up with her, I like her.'

"Within thirty days, Samantha had broken up with her boyfriend, and I had everything to do with it. My cousin, or evil twin, worked her magic. Justine talked me up to Samantha and gave me Sam's cell number. I called. We spoke and texted a couple more times after that, and in a few days, we met up. We met up a couple more times and were getting a feel for each other. The chemistry was there. I told her, 'Sam, you gotta get rid of this kid.' Samantha was a girl with true character. When I posed the prospect of her leaving her boyfriend of three years, she laid all her cards on the table.

"Samantha knew I was a player around town, partying most nights, dating the hottest women, and seeing several women at once. She said it and told me straight, 'I'm not going to leave him when I know you're running around.' "I said, 'I'm done with that, Sam. I want you in my life.' "Sam believed me. She would break up with the dude she was seeing, and our relationship would escalate. As time passed, one by one, I would break up with the women I was seeing. To be honest, my plan was to sleep with Sam for a while and then break up with her. Yep, I'm a prick like that.

"Sam would wind up holding all the cards because I fell in love with her. We both fell in love. The reality was simple: she was the only woman I wanted to be with.

"As time passed, Samantha and I grew closer and closer. When hurricane Sandy struck, my apartment was flooded, and I moved into a vacant apartment at Samantha's mother's house. Sam still lived at home with her mother. Sam's mother was Lisa. Yes, the same Lisa that Ronnie was supposed to beat to death with a pipe in front of her own house. Lisa, Samantha, and their family members that would stop over at the house became my second family. Lisa and I became extremely close. We would text each other and enjoyed each other's company.

"Ronnie would eventually learn that Sam's mother was the woman Joe Massino wanted dead. I don't know why, but it was something he could never move past. Because of Lisa, he wanted me to break up with Samantha.

"Around this time, as part of our daily routine, Ronnie and I utilized a personal trainer. Three times a week ,we would go to Gold's Gym to work out, and Claudia would meet us, bringing a custom protein drink for her trainees. Claudia was seven years older than me and ripped to shreds. She was a divorcee with two kids, she had her own home, and was a responsible and loving mother. When I looked at Claudia, she reminded me of Gwen Stefani with absolutely no body fat. I would come to learn from Tish, Ronnie's wife, that after Claudia's divorce, she hadn't slept with anyone for several years. Though I was living in Samantha's house and we were in love, Claudia and I got closer and closer. Before I knew it, Claudia and I had fallen in love. It was real, just as real as the love I experienced with Samantha.

"I was absolutely and unequivocally torn between these two women. Of all the shit I've been through in my life, this situation was the one I could not deal with. No matter my choice, I would hurt the woman I loved. A grown man, twenty-nine years old, I was so perplexed with what to do, I stopped over at my mother's house for advice. My mother told me what I knew all along. 'You're in a bad spot.'

"To add to this maddening problem, Ronnie inserted himself into the equation. You see, your Mafia superiors oftentimes have a say in the woman you are with. Not so much these days, but old school Mafiosi, like Ronnie, will assert themselves and impose their will. Ronnie was right in the middle of the affair. All along, Ronnie had been pushing me to break up with Samantha. His one and only reason was Sam's mother, Lisa. He was being extremely manipulative in how he was going about it. He started with not giving me money to put on the street. When I asked him why, he said, 'You have to slow down a little.' Ronnie not making money didn't compute. Next, we're having a conversation about an apartment. Ronnie had already rented a two-bedroom apartment. When he couldn't convince me to move from Samantha's apartment, he began to insist. Ronnie was adamant that Samantha and I should not be together. He was trying everything within his power, and his power was considerable, to persuade me, with no effect. Last was the ultimatum: Ronnie said, 'You gotta choose, her or us. Her family is no good, get away from them.'

"This was beyond all belief; I'm juggling two love interests, I don't want to hurt either, and Ronnie is forcing me to choose between the girl or the mob. I couldn't handle it. I was sitting on a quarter million in cash; I pointed south and headed to Florida. Seventeen hours later, I was there, free from all the bullshit. Samantha and I rented a beach front apartment in Miami and partied. I don't remember all the details; some of this period is a blur.

"When we left, virtually no one knew we were gone, not even Ronnie. I was gone for three weeks, and I was not tending to Ronnie's empire. He could do it his fuckin' self. When I headed south with Sam, I was mentally overwhelmed; even so, the fog was beginning to clear. Being in Miami with Sam, I was able to begin to explore my options. Realistically, I didn't need Ronnie. Access to his money made things easier but it came with many strings.

"I needed Ronnie to put me up for my button.

"He seemed to resent that those in the know in our area feared me, and I had won the respect of Mafioso from other crime families. I had achieved my position despite Ronnie's presence. At this point, he was holding me back, probably to maintain his business and to have me remain his enforcer.

"Bouncing all these thoughts around in my head, my path was clear: I knew I had but one choice.

"I would have to kill Ronnie. It would have to be done on the sneak, and all motives would have to be elsewhere. Because I had such intimate knowledge of his business, I could easily move in and take over his sports and loan action. Had Ronnie been killed, an investigation would have ensued. The Bonanno family would need to know what happened and why. I would have had to make it look like a robbery gone bad. As far as the guys in Ronnie's crew, the majority of them would have secretly been celebrating. I had convinced myself this was my only way forward.

"There was one problem, and it was huge. The criminal in me knew I had to kill him, but the responsible side could not hurt his family, who I had come to love dearly. His family literally saved his life.

"My choice was Samantha. All my money-making activity with Ronnie ceased. For the most part, we were done. I continued to travel back and forth to Miami; when in New York, I would see Claudia to catch up with her. This would last for seven months.

"Finally, the bill would come due. While driving to Mike Pecchio's wedding, the law swarmed, and my life of crime came to an abrupt and final end."

GOING TOO FAR

There is a well-known story about a particularly infamous gangster out of Chicago by the name of Tony Spilotro, a made guy with the Chicago Outfit. Spilotro was made famous in the blockbuster movie Casino. He was played by Joe Pesci.

Spilotro went to dinner with a couple of guys, probably part of his crew. When the check for the meal arrived, he signed the check "Crime." He told the waiter, "And crime don't pay." Spilotro was put in Las Vegas by the Chicago Outfit, but he quickly got out of control. Chicago ordered his death. Even by mob standards, he was killed badly. Taken out to a cornfield, Tony and his brother were beaten with baseball bats and buried alive. Spilotro thought his member status gave him a blank check to rob and murder at his whim. But it didn't. He paid the ultimate price for going too far.

In the mob, there is a pecking order. Even as an associate, if you are not perceived as a dangerous guy, it is very easy to become dead. Those often perceived as weak are the guys who are usually earners. Money and the criminal organization is what gives a gangster strength. Among the membership, a guy has to be liked and/ or respected (a killer) or have a very close circle of friends or family to keep him untouched by the predators. This is what made Vinny Asaro so strong: his whole family was deeply involved with Mafia life, and most were dangerous.

But the earner is more concerned with making money that having a body count is resented by those who came up through the ranks old school. These days, a guy will get a button and never have done a real piece of work, a killing.

Today, they become members strictly for their earning potential.

A Bonanno crew member named Bam was proposed to become a member; it was a done deal, he was going to be made. The guy was so excited, he told a couple of his friend. It got back to the membership and would be postponed. Getting a button was probably the highlight of Bam's life.

Bam was a very wealthy guy, a multimillionaire without a doubt, for sure. He started young, in his twenties, and kept building and building and building.

Borrello explains the Bam story: "The biggest auto

body shop in Queens was owned by Bam. The garage was huge. It had its own spray booth and five bays.

"The property was so large, Bam was renting out the other half to other mechanics and automotive-related businesses. This enterprise wasn't his only business. Bam was also running a sports book, but nothing compared to Ronnie G's. Bam, at one point, was wholesaling money at half a point to his guys. When Ronnie G heard about the price, he called Bam in and told him, 'You put out money at a point, no less.' It was an order, and Bam had no choice but to comply. On another occasion, he was lending money to Gambino guys, and Uncle Vin had a big problem with it. Vin knew it would cause problems down the road. Bam was lending hundreds of thousands to the Gambino family; should he get stiffed, it could cause serious repercussions.

"When the Ferrari 458 came out, he went and bought one that week. Then the following week or so, the Ferrari 458 convertible came out, and before he could sell the first Ferrari, he had a second. He spent seven hundred thousand on cars in a few weeks, and he had a Bentley, an Aston Martin, and other exotic cars. Bam was a good guy. With me, he was generous, respectful, even though he was twenty years older than me. When a guy is that successful, he will have his share of haters. To add insult to injury, he was with Jerry Asaro, a Bonanno captain. Answering to a captain, other guys actually get jealous, the same way they were jealous of me because I answered to Ronnie G, and more so when Ronnie went away and I answered to Uncle Vin. Though Bam was with Jerry when he sent his monthly envelope, John Ragano would pick it up and give it to Jerry.

"Bam had John Ragano working for him to satisfy his parole officer, as a favor to Jerry. Bam was paying Ragano a thousand a week. To do what, I have no idea.

"John Ragano, a member, and Bald Chris were no fans of Bam. Chris had called me to come and meet him and John at a diner down the block from Bam's garage on Liberty Avenue. I headed over to the diner; John and Chris were already there. I went in and saw them sitting in the booth. The place wasn't very crowded; the lunch rush had already passed. I sat with them and said, 'What's goin' on?'

"John does the talking; he leans in to me and, in a hushed voice, explained, 'Listen I'm bringing this to you because we know you can be trusted and we know you do scores. Bam is a greedy fuck, I don't like him. He's a jerkoff, a real clown. We want you to hit his house. He's gonna have three hundred thousand comin' from Vinny Carwash, but fifty is goin' somewhere else, and he's being paid 130,000 dollars from 'Johnny Beano,' but that's goin' to Uncle Vin and Tommy, plus any jewelry and whatever else you get. We'll know when he's paid, and we'll let you know.'

"John further instructed, "The only time the house can be hit is when the cleaning woman is home because you won't be able to beat the alarm system. Someone lets her in, then they lock the door till she leaves.'

"I was listening intently as John explained everything. When he paused, I mumbled aloud to myself, 'So we gotta do a home invasion, John?'

"'What?'

"I said, 'Nothin, I'm thinking out loud.'

"'Oh, we got the key to the front door.'

"'Sounds good, I'll wait for your call,' I replied. At that, we parted company.

"My mind was racing. I began digesting everything I

was told, factored in everything I knew about Bam, and realized this could be a million-dollar job. There was no telling what valuables Bam had in his house. From that moment, it was a waiting game.

"All I had to do was make a couple of phone calls to make

sure my guys were ready. I had figured I would hear from John or Chris in a week or two. Nothing. A couple months passed, and the next thing I know, John Ragano is locked up with a bunch of others on the Lufthansa Heist. I figured the Bam score was dead.

"Another two months passed, and I'm in Florida living the high life, and Bald Chris called. He said, 'I need you.'

"'For what?'

"'Auto body.'

"'I'm in Florida, when?' "'Tomorrow morning.'

"'Don't worry, I'll send one of my guys.' "'I trust you.'

"I called Fat Matt, telling him, 'I need you tomorrow.'

"Fat Matt asked, 'It's gotta be tomorrow?'

"'Yeah.'

"Fat Matt replied, 'I gotta be somewhere tomorrow. I can't get out of it.' "I said, 'Alright, don't worry about it, I'll get somebody.' "As soon as I hung up the phone with Fat Matt, I called my cousin, Frank Nunziata. Calling Frankie was a stretch; he was the only game in town. He had never done a home invasion before, and I didn't have complete faith in him. The only upside was that he would be partnered with Mac. Mac was a pro when it came to home invasions. I called Frankie and said, 'Frankie, whattaya doing? Ya wanna make some money?'

"Frankie yells, 'Yeah.'

"'All right, listen, you have to be up early tomorrow, you're gonna go with Mac. You listen to everything he says, no questions, and do it. I'm gonna give you his number, and I'll let him know you're gonna call; he'll tell you where to meet him, and you bring a car.'

"Once I ended the call with Frankie, I had a couple of things to do that would take maybe an hour or so, and then I would be on the road. Samantha took the ride with me. I don't fly unless there is no alternative -deathly afraid. I don't drive out of necessity, I love it. Spending sixteen, eighteen hours behind the wheel is a pleasure. While en route, I get a call from Frankie at about 7:00 a.m. He told me, 'Gene, I'm here with Mac.'

"'All right.'

"'Okay, see ya.'

"I said, 'Frankie, one more thing...as soon as you're done, you call me.'

"They had the key; the job should go smoothly.

"When they entered the house, they surprised Bam's girlfriend lying on the couch, zip tied her, and went to work. They found 250,000 dollars in cash and 125,000 dollars in jewelry once it was fenced.

"Frankie followed my instructions; as soon as they left the house, Frankie called me.

"'Gene.'

"'Good?'

"'Yeah.'

"'A lot?'

"'Yeah.'

"'All right, shut up, I'll be there at about eight tonight. Listen, you hold everything...everything, until I get there.'

"'Gotcha.'

"I settled in and enjoyed the ride. It was nice knowing I'd have a big payday and didn't have to do anything. Knowing Samantha the way that I do, in her mind, she was planning a big, expensive night out.

"As soon as we arrived in Howard Beach, I went over to Frankie's house to collect the goods. It was a nice haul, exactly what we expected. From there, Samantha and I checked into a hotel on Queens Boulevard. I didn't want to be seen in the neighborhood; I would be blamed, and later on, I was.

"I laid everything out; counting the cash was easy - twenty-five packs of ten grand, all new, blue hundreds. A cool quarter million. There was also a watch winder box, which meant highend watches. There were five or six watches, but I knew their retail value was about three hundred thousand.

"With everything counted, I called Bald Chris to let him know where I was and to come over. When we spoke, he mentioned he was bringing his buddy; I knew who he meant.

About a half hour later, Bald Chris and Andrew Curro showed up. We discussed dividing the money; it's a four way split: Andrew Curro and John Ragano get a share, Bald Chris a share, Mac a share, and Frankie and I take a share. No problem. Nobody asked about the watches. Bald Chris and I would fence them later and get sixty thousand apiece. Once we divided the cash, Andrew and I had to have a conversation.

"Andrew had to tell me word was going around that my cousin, Joey Borrello, The Ginerbread Man, was a rat. Joey wasn't around mob guys. and in that respect, he wasn't a threat, but Andrew liked me and wanted to make sure I was all right. As soon as Andrew told me, I responded, 'Who said it?'

"Andrew replied, 'Dutch,' Joey's and my first cousin. "I asked him, 'What ya doing with Dutch?' "Andrew said, 'I'm gettin large amounts of weed off him.'

"'Let me stop you right there; Joey's not a rat. Before you put a jerk-off like that around you, Jerry Bruno used to slap Dutch around and extort him for twenty-five hundred a week."

"Andrew replied, 'Enough said, I got you.'

"'He's an embarrassment to us; me and Joey would never be abused like that. Don't let Dutch fool you.' The Gingerbread Man conversation was done. Joey served time in prison five times, ran from the cops every time; he was a criminal through and through, and if he went to jail, it was because he was literally caught.

"Andrew and I were close; there was mutual respect.

191

To Andrew, I was a kid; he was twenty-seven years my senior. Andrew and I talked freely with one and other. While we were making small talk between the three of us, Andrew asked me, 'How you gettin' along with Ronnie?'

"'I'm hatin' him right now.' "'You and me both.'

"'Really?'

"'Me, John, and Jerry can't stand him.'

"'That's funny you say that, my good buddy. Todd LaBarca told me you gotta get away from him; he's one of the most hated guys around.'

"We were both laughing. I never realized how disliked Ronnie G was. Then Andrew said, 'Well, where's he keep it?' meaning Ronnie's cash.

"'He's too smart for that; he keeps it all in safety deposit boxes.'

"Andrew laughed and said, 'Yeah, there's no way.' And he continued on saying, 'I got a tip on a big score in Long Island, half-a million. My guy just saw it with his own eyes; it's good, but you gotta move fast.' Moving fast didn't give us the opportunity to do the proper leg work. In fact, we may have jumped the gun.

"It was one of those jobs where everything that could go wrong did. I'll skip the details...we gained entry, the wife was secured on the first floor.

"Mac started up the stairs, and the husband was standing at the top of the stairs with a gun pointed at his chest. The guy could have easily killed Mac, but he chose not to shoot. The guy was a loan shark, and my guess is the gun was unregistered and he didn't want the headache. Sometimes you walked away with cash in your pockets, sometimes the job got botched, and sometimes, the other guy wins.

"Once this job went bad, Samantha and I drove south to our apartment in Florida. Being in Florida, having cash to live the good life, beautiful girl on my arm who I happened to love, it really doesn't get much better. Sam and I would travel to and from New York about once a month. If it wasn't for the money, I would've come back every three months. I, my world, my life, was good.

"In other corners, though, others have their own agendas, and while I'm living it up, they're grinding away at what they do. And they are good at it, fuckin' pros. Sam and I make one of our monthly trips to New York to attend an event, and I'm taken by compete surprise; I got arrested.

"The arrest came out of nowhere. Nothing added up, I couldn't wrap my head around why. During my arraignment, everything became clear. I was arrested by Queens County Organized Crime Task Force and charged with all state charges. The arrest was the first nail in my coffin. Several months later on the Gangland website, they released a story on the Bam home invasion.

"The website reported that John Ragano recruited me to rob Bam. And they were saying there was a federal indictment. I knew the website was full of shit. I'm looking at papers charging me with all state crimes. Two weeks passed, and Florida filed charges against me. They were state charges for a robbery I did down there. It was a decent job, forty thousand. This was getting...serious. Bam was Jerry Asaro's guy; if it was a fact that I did it, I would have to answer for the robbery. This was another nail in my coffin. There would be more pressure, much more.

"When I think about the times I had gone too far in the past, aside from the Bam home invasion, one incident comes to mind. I was arguing with Darren while he was driving his mother's car. We were going back and forth aggressively. The argument got so heated, I drew a pistol, wanting to shoot him, but I shot the car. The car limped on for a couple of blocks and died.

"The point being, I lived in world where I gave orders and people followed them. Only a couple of guys could give me orders. I was a gangster, and I was untouchable. That mindset would lead to my undoing, for all too often, I would be going too far."

VISITS

Believing the feds were not involved was a misstep for Borrello. Maybe false hope. Dealing with the state is one thing, but the feds don't waste resources; when they come, they come hard. Borrello was appointed David Guy to represent him. Being a criminal attorney, Guy was seeing things clearly. Once Borrello was arraigned, Guy had said he knew it was a wire-tap case by the way Borrello was being charged.

Borrello was being charged with a home invasion that never took place; in fact, he was in Florida when Frank Nunziata and Borrello's brother got stopped while in transit to do the home invasion.

During the arraignment, when the charging document was read, the Assistant District Attorney stated Frank Nunziata was providing information.

Borrello recounts, "There were three things I was concerned about: Frank getting rid of the gun I used to shoot Luigi, Bam's home invasion, and another home invasion.

"Two weeks later, I was being charged with a robbery in Florida. One of the arresting officers, Jerry McNeely, a state OCTF cop, had said something that was eating at me. I had asked him, 'What am I a suspect in?'

"With an emotionless face, McNeely said, 'Everything.'

"I was taken by surprise and had no response to speak of.

"McNeely continued, 'And we'll be back again and again

and again.'

"Two weeks after that, my attorney came to visit Rikers. He had been saying all along that the feds were involved; he knew how they operated. To make matters worse, my attorney believed there were multiple witnesses, meaning cooperators, against me. Throughout our interactions, he suggested that I cooperate. As of yet, the federal government never showed up. They were state cases and nothing more. Three months after my arrest, David, my attorney, got a call from the Assistant United States Attorney's Office to shed some light on my situation. Being an ex-ADA of twenty-five years, David figured someone may offer some sound advice. The next time he saw me, he told me about the call. David never said who he spoke to, but he made it clear: 'They want you to cooperate.' Cooperating was not an option.

"Eight months in, and a couple more things unfolded. The Gangland website released an article talking about me as a crew leader; I was doing home invasions, and it specifically fingered me for Bam's home invasion, saying I was working with John Ragano, and went on to compare my crimes to the movie, 'Rob The Mob,' where the thieves were ultimately murdered. The following week, my attorney, having previously filed for discovery, received ten thousand pages of wire-tap transcripts with at least eighty percent of the information redacted. Between the article, the redacted wiretap transcripts, and my lawyer telling me the feds were involved, it was a lot to think about. I had someone print the Gangland article. When I read it, I had to believe the feds had something to do with its content. Thought they'll never admit it, I'm sure there was a confidential source.

"Once the article came out, everything seemed to go quiet for a while. A couple of months later, I got a visit from Frank 'Bones' Caputo. He conveyed a message from Ronnie and some in formation about the family. Ronnie had said he would kick in thirty thousand, should a federal indictment issue arise. The second piece of information was very interesting. Ronnie and Anthony Pepitone were trying to take over the family, Ronnie as the acting boss and Anthony as the acting underboss. The vacancy was due to Tommy DiFiore going to jail. Uncle Vin was Tommy's guiding hand, but Vin didn't want the top spot...too much attention. I figured Vin was pushing Ronnie to become acting boss, for one day he may actually be the boss. That was some excitement.

It lasted about a second. Jail is nothing but monotony; coming off the street, being in the midst of all the action of leading a gangster's life and lifestyle, to being relegated to a tier. A fucking tier; same people, same routine. Fights and stabbings every day. The change was dramatic.

"Members of the Bonanno task force, three guys, came to visit me one week before Christmas, 2015. I was in my cell. I looked up, and I saw a female in a white shirt, and she told me, 'Borrello, you got a visit.' This was abnormal; there was no visiting at 9:00 a.m. on that particular day. I asked the captain in a hushed tone, 'Who is it, the feds?' "The captain confirmed my statement with a discreet nod. "She unlocked my cell and escorted me to the front desk, where I was cuffed behind my back. Once cuffed, three plainclothes correctional officers took me out of the building to a trailer where three men were waiting.

Entering the trailer, the cuffs were removed, I was offered a seat, and we settled in for a conversation.

"I thought the walk would have taken longer; hell, Rikers Island had fourteen thousand prisoners -it's more populated than most American towns. Yet, it seemed like I took a few steps, and I was sitting in front of these guys, and I knew the questions they would ask. I've never pondered this moment, though I knew it was coming...you can never fully prepare yourself for life-changing decisions. For all the dangerous situations I've been in throughout my life -arguments, robberies, fights, stabbings, shootings -this situation was where I was most nervous.

"Sitting down, they introduced themselves. Rob and Adam were federal agents who worked the Bonanno crime family. The third guy introduced himself, but for the life of me, I cannot remember his name. His concern was homicides. I'm guessing he was a detective who worked organized crime-related murders. They were gentlemanly and cordial enough. As my mind was racing, I'm waiting for the question. How do you go literally from a life of crime, around some of the most notorious gangsters in the mob, to a rat? When my mind slowed a little, I realized I knew Rob and Adam because I had seen them on the front page of all the New York papers when Uncle Vin was arrested for the Lufthansa Heist.

"At the right time, they eased into their reason for being there. Adam spoke very directly:

"'Do you want to strike first?' They went on to explain that they work Howard Beach every day. 'We know what's going on, and they don't have your back anymore. If you want to move forward, sign if you want to cooperate.' The document had to do with granting them permission to obtain a court-appointed attorney to represent me through the process of cooperation. My mind was racing again; there's never enough time when making decisions of that magnitude. My passing thoughts were to protect my brother, my ex-girlfriend dying in prison, and Ronnie G, my once friend and mentor. Our relationship was done, and prior to my arrest, I was contemplating killing him. Before I knew it, I heard myself saying, 'Fuck it, give me the paper.' They slid the document to me, I signed, and my life as a criminal was over with the stroke of a pen.

"For Christmas, 2015, I became a federal witness. I could have thought of thousands of presents I would have preferred. I told the agents, 'Listen, you need to make sure it isn't leaked about my cooperation. I'm in a maximum security unit with serious guys…if they think for a second I'm cooperating, I'm getting cut up.'

"Rikers Island was complete chaos. I don't have the words to describe the madness. People got cut and stabbed every day for meaningless slights. I had to be sure I gave a good reason for being taken out. When I got to the block, I explained to the guys that I was pulled out for questioning. My story was readily accepted because of recent articles and the nature of the case. I was content; no one knew I ratted for the time being.

"Just because I was locked up, the world goes on, even the criminal world.

"A couple weeks later at a Christmas party, the new

Bonanno boss, Joe Cammarano, would meet many of his family and receive envelopes. It's a party for the Mafia, all captains and above, but each must bring a soldier to introduce his captain to others. It's political ceremony. And when introduced to the boss, he's handed an envelope with cash as tribute. From my faction, there was Ronnie G, Mike Padavona, and Uncle Vin; from the Queens, Middle Village, faction, Anthony Pepitone and his soldier all met with Joe. Come the middle of January, Ronnie G and Anthony Pepitone all violated the conditions of their supervised release. By February, the both of them would be back in prison. Their violation was for meeting with a known Mafia member. Ronnie would receive one year, and Anthony two years.

"So far, I was still in a position to back out of cooperating because I had not provided any information. Nah, I joined Team America. I was committed to saving my life and helping those I care for. The second week of January, I heard the C.O. hollering my name, 'Borrello Court!'

"It wasn't court, it was the feds. Round two. I was anxious, but ready. I was being written out and placed in the custody of the F.B.I. The agents were familiar: Adam and Rob from the first meeting, and also the homicide detective, who shall remain nameless because I cannot remember his fucking name.

"During the ride, we made small talk, nothing in particular. Twenty minutes later, we were in the federal building in Brooklyn. I was taken to a small conference room. I sat down, and they handcuffed me to the chair. The agents and detective stayed with me, and I met Nancy Anise for the first time. The government had her appointed as counsel to represent me throughout the debriefing process and court proceedings. Before the government's attorneys arrived, the agents and detective excused themselves so I could speak privately with my attorney. Nancy basically walked me through the entire process of debriefing: answer all their questions, don't lie. Nancy explained to me that she had worked with the office before, specifically with Nicole Argentieri, who was very fair. Maybe ten minutes passed, and everyone was ready to sit down and meet.

"The room quickly filled: Adam, Rob, the city detective, Allison Coolie, Lindsay Gerdes, and Nicole Argentieri. They all settled in around the conference table. Nicole was the boss. It was clear from the way they spoke to her and the way she carried herself with an air of confidence and authority. There were introductions all around.

"Nicole immediately asked to have me un-cuffed. Rob responded, telling Nicole, 'I can't; it's a new procedure.'

"The questioning started. Basically, I had to tell my entire life story. We spoke about all of my family, who were actual gangsters, who were affiliated, and so forth. Everything I talk about in this book, and so much more, was discussed. The city detective went through a list of unsolved murders in my area and asked me if I had killed anybody. I answered, 'No.' After that, the detective didn't attend any future debriefing sessions, but the questions about murders were asked five or six times. My guess is that cooperators don't want to admit to the most serious crime and instead, accuse another of murder; someone they debrief on thinking that person will never cooperate and it bites the witness and the government right in the ass.

"The government has the process of obtaining cooperating witnesses down to a science. There was a time when the process was not so straight forward. But now, when done properly, it has become a win-win proposition. It benefits the defendant and the government. The wheels of justice continue to turn."

COOPERATING WITNESS

The process of recruiting cooperating witnesses is still evolving and will continue to evolve, even though the federal government is now very adroit at it.

There are occasions where there are reasonable misunderstandings, usually the result of tacit promises. Or, a potential witness will be led to believe he will receive a sentence more lenient than the one imposed.

Federal agents, detectives, and police officers have no authority, whatsoever, to promise leniency, a specific sentence, or anything else to lower sentences. Many criminals are duped into incriminating themselves, and it just gets worse from there. Once the cat is out of the bag, it is virtually impossible to undo what has been attested to.

For decades past, the process of a plea deal was looked at as unscrupulous because deals were hashed out in smoke-filled back rooms. The process, as it then existed, gave the appearance of impropriety. When something was not in the public eye, there is a temptation to believe wrongdoing exists. Let's say a moneyed drug dealer hires a top lawyer to represent him, someone known to have ties to the District Attorney's Office, and the drug dealer is facing thirty years. His attorney approaches the dealer with egofilled promises, 'Listen, I play golf with the ADA every Saturday. I can get him to give you a plea deal for ten years, but I'll need another hundred thousand.' The additional money gives the appearance the ADA is being paid off. In reality, maybe the lawyer pocketed the money, maybe he slipped an envelope into the ADA's golf bag, or maybe when the ADA leaves public practice, the high-priced lawyer guarantees him a job with an enticing starting salary at his law firm. All of the possibilities are realistic, and they certainly may have all occurred in the past. Fortunately, as the process has evolved, it did so in such a way to discourage corruption and bring the plea-bargaining process into the light.

The plea negotiation that ultimately leads to a plea agreement is reduced to writing and had become a matter of public record because it is submitted to the court. There are three parties to any plea agreement: the prosecution, the defense, and the court. Make no mistake, every party must be in agreement about the outcome. Should the court not accept the agreement, a defendant could be forced to trial. While this is quite possible, it rarely occurs. Most judges tend to cooperate with the ADA's and the United States Attorney's offices.

Like plea bargaining, the process of obtaining cooperation has also evolved. Prior to1987, the federal government, to secure cooperation, would employ "charge bargaining" to make a deal. As an example: a defendant may be charged with a murder. The A.U.S.A.,[12] though, believes he wasn't the shooter. While equally culpable, the A.U.S.A. may say, "my office will drop the charge to voluntary manslaughter if you testify." A reduced charge is "money" in this game.

After 1987, everything changed, and it changed dramatically. The Federal Rules of Criminal Procedure amended Rule 35(b). It went from a post-sentencing

---

[12] Assistant United States Attorney

motion filed by the defendant requesting leniency to a motion filed by the United State Attorney's Office based on "substantial assistance" by the defendant.

A United States Sentencing Guideline 5kl.l was written in lockstep with the Rule 35(b). The difference was the timing. A 5kl.l "letter" submitted to the sentencing court would allow thecourt to depart below the sentencing guidelines during the imposition of the initial sentence. The Rule 35(b) was to reduce an already imposed sentence based on the government's motion.

This law and sentencing guideline placed greater and significant power in the hands of an Assistant United States Attorney. Previously, an A.U.S.A. had the authority to promise a sentence in a plea agreement. Even without cooperation, they could charge bargain or reduce the charge against a defendant, or they could simply choose not to prosecute. The new landscape gave the federal prosecutor the best of both worlds.

The key element of the guideline and the rule is "substantial assistance." It is based solely upon the prosecutor's subjective determination whether a cooperating witness provided substantial assistance. The sentencing guidelines, without consideration for a substantial assistance, are first determined by the pre-sentence report. A defendant could be facing guidelines with a range of 20 to 27 years without cooperation.

With cooperation, normally, there will be a fifty percent reduction of the minimum. In Borrello's case, ten years. Fifty percent is the average reduction for a normal level of cooperation. Lower and higher percentages occur contingent upon the level of cooperation, some as high as eighty-five percent, and some as low as five percent.

Borrello knew what was potentially happening to him. "Had I not cooperated, between state and federal

charges, a plea deal for thirty years would have been a bargain. The respective governments would have been throwing me a lifeline. I was thirty when I was arrested. I would have been in my early sixties when finally released.

"As a one-time organized criminal, I can say once you are on the radar of the F.B.I., your criminal career is nearing an end."

JOEY RUSSO

"Once I signed the document allowing the government to obtain counsel in the middle of December, 2015, and after three debriefing sessions, I was immediately transferred from Rikers Island to Somerset County, New Jersey. They put me under the cover name as Joseph Russo.

"The change was dramatic. After nineteen months at the hell-hole Rikers, I actually became accustomed to the fights and stabbings nearly every day, unscheduled lockdowns, and the overall chaos in general. By contrast, Somerset County was full of heroin addicts, forty guys to a pod, very subdued. Me arriving there was like putting a great white shark

amid a cove of swimmers. Within a couple of weeks, I had the run of the pod. Being under an alias was comforting, but in this jail, if they knew I was cooperating, it would mean nothing. The worst part about being at this jail was there was virtually no yard to get fresh air. The best part was the food.

"There was no comparison - Rikers was like eating at a homeless shelter, and Somerset County was like eating at Peter Luger's steak house.

"The third debriefing session was my last time in Rikers Island. It was April, 2016, and I was called for 'court' once again. Usually when the agents, Rob and Adam, would pick me up for court, they would be driving a car; this time, though, they had a Suburban. The two AUSAs were also in the truck. Based on all that I had debriefed on up to that point, they had to drive to all the crime scenes to see the physical layouts as I explained once again how the events unfolded. When we were done, the federal agents dropped off Allison Coolie and Lindsay Gerdes at the federal building, and we traveled about ninety minutes to Somerset County, New Jersey.

"Approximately every two weeks, I was being taken out for further debriefing. Rob and Adam always were the agents to transport me. We would go to a federal building in Jersey, about a ten-minute drive from the jail. The sessions would last from eight a.m. to three in the afternoon. Basically, we discussed my entire life of crime for the past fourteen years, starting with my first arrest when I was sixteen and moving forward in time and my progression as a criminal.

"As I said before, most of the crimes were already mentioned, but the process in and of itself was fascinating. Nicole Argentieri, the lead prosecutor on the case, was meticulous with details. When she already knew the answers to the question posed, she would have me answer in vivid detail. At that time, I thought she was being a hardass; in retrospect, she was being a thorough prosecutor. As the level of trust grew between us, questions were posed asking my opinion. Many of the conversations we had would unfold in the media, and exactly what I had said came to pass. One day, I was discussing with Nicole how much time she should offer Ronnie to get him to accept a plea and the fine. I suggested to Nicole a sentence between twelve and fifteen years and a two million dollar fine. He actually received a fourteen-year sentence and a one point two million-dollar fine.

"That made me realize how closely they listened during

our debriefing sessions. Especially when we would have a discussion, and a few days later, I would see an article by a crime reporter writing my words, but coming from the government.

"When we talked about Uncle Vin, I told Nicole he was the only one that would go to trial. Sure enough, Vin wanted a trial. And he wanted a speedy trial. At that time, Uncle Vin was eighty-two. Any sentence would be a death sentence, but the government only charged Vin with an arson, and sweetened the pot by offering a zeroto twenty-year sentencing guideline range. Vin also received credit of twenty-two months towards whatever sentence would be imposed in the future because of the time he had served in jail for the Lufthansa Heist case where he was acquitted. Vin figured, at his age, twenty-two months credit, and whatever time he already served in jail, once he took the deal and was sentenced, he would be home in no time. Judge Ross didn't see it quite that way. She sentenced Vin to fifteen years and had commented that she believed he was responsible for murders, the Lufthansa Heist, and was still ordering underlings to commit crimes.

"Nick 'Pudgie' Festa was sentenced to six years. A skid bit in prison parlance. When he submitted his appeal to receive bail, he had a laundry list of forty crimes I committed; some I debriefed on, and some I didn't. There was no way I remembered all the crimes I committed. Pudgie's allegations, when he said I attempted to shoot Chris Cognata in a restaurant, was a blunder. When the agent told me about it, I said, 'He can get in trouble for that with Ronnie.'

"Rob said, 'It's funny you say that; Nicole said the same

thing.'

"The nut had no clue he was indirectly ratting on Ronnie by confirming my debriefing on the matter.

"Several debriefing sessions later, I was asked with specificity about the house Ronnie built. Later, it became a bigger deal than I had ever expected. Let's face it, Ronnie had a job earning thirty-seven thousand dollars a year. Maybe he showed more legitimate income, but I have no idea where it might have come from. This three-million-dollar house was Ronnie spitting in the eye of the government. Part of his sentencing ordered the sale of the house. Quite simply, the United States Attorney's Office would not allow Ronnie to keep that house under any circumstances.

"Nicole Argentieri pressed this issue to the max.

She was mentor to Lindsay Gerdes, who would often question me when Nicole was dealing with other matters. Lindsay had a more amiable personality, but like Nicole, she was very professional.

"During the debriefing process while at Somerset County jail, I was involved in an incident. Actually, a couple of incidents. A new arrival was put in our pod of forty-plus guys. I said to my friend and roommate, Black, 'This guy's gonna be a problem.' Sure enough, I called good money. The guy, Boogs, was a Blood gang member, and he had a problem with the way extra food was being distributed. Any extra trays were being rotated among the guys on a fair basis; eventually, everybody got an extra tray. It was my job to distribute the food. Boogs's problem was that he wanted an extra tray every single day. It wasn't happening.

"At about two weeks, Boogs had words with my roommate Black. Boogs yelled at Black publicly, 'Suck my dick.' Black went up the stairs to go to Boogs's cell. They started fighting in the cell. I got there about thirty seconds to a minute behind Black.

They were goin' at it. Black was getting the better of him. I stood and watched for a bit, then intervened and broke it up. Black and I left. After a few minutes, I didn't see Boogs come out of the cell and went to check on him. I asked him, 'You all right?'

"Boogs told me, 'Yeah, yeah I'm good, man.' I went back to check on the guy a couple more times. Once he complained he had chest pains. The last time he was passed out. I threw a bucket of water on him so he would wake up, no good. When he didn't wake up, I hit the call button. Over the intercom, a voice said, 'What's wrong?'

"'This guy's got heart problems,' I yelled.

"Medical came; they assessed the situation. They immediately began chest compressions, then shocked him with the paddles, put him on a stretcher and rushed him to the hospital. Boogs died at the hospital several hours later. The autopsy would show he had high levels of synthetic heroin (suboxin) in his system and died from an overdose. But it wasn't over yet. The family would protest outside the jail. And social media, being what it is, all hell broke loose.

"The feedback we were hearing from our families

watching social media was crazy. They were saying Black and I beat the guy to death in his cell, then we started hearing the same from the guys on the pod. And they were praising us because as it turned out, most guys in the jail hated Boogs. And social media showed he wasn't too well liked on the street. Actually, I'm being kind. He was hated on the street as well as in the jail. He was a straight-up predator and opportunist. Knowing both of them, he was nothing more than a black Chris Cognata, who eventually got what he deserved.

"Life before the pod remained calm. There were no incidents to speak of, which is good, not just for me, but for everyone. It makes the correctional officers' jobs easier, and they don't bother us when everything is peaceful, and it makes it easier for all the guys doing time.

"November, 2016, seemed to arrive sooner than expected. I would be pleading guilty in the federal building in the Easter District of New York in Brooklyn. The crimes I pleaded guilty to were:
• Conspiracy to commit murder;
• Attempt to commit murder with a firearm;
• Racketeering, assault, conspiracy;
• Arson;
• Loansharking and gambling;
• Hobbs Act robbery.

"Once all these charges were read, the judge told me the guidelines. I was facing fifteen to life imprisonment. Hearing that, even as a cooperating witness, I was upset. There's always that chance, though you don't want to believe it, that you're being tricked. It was unsettling. Her honor went on to explain how she arrived at fifteen to life.

She said I was receiving a minimum of ten years for all the charges except arson; the arson charge would be five years to run consecutive to the ten years, and life was because of the attempted murder for a criminal organization.

"That was a big step, maybe just a formality, but it made everything official. A few weeks passed, and I was taken from the prison. This time, no debriefing, I was given a lie-detector test to determine if I would be accepted into Phase I (prison) of the Witness Protection Program. I passed. Now I was just waiting.

"During that period, on Easter Sunday of all days, a new arrival was using the phone. The guy sneezed on the phone. We all used the phones, so I asked the guy, 'We all use the phone, could you do me a favor and wipe it off?'

"The guy said with attitude, 'I ain't cleaning it up, you clean it up.'

"For a few seconds, I didn't pay it any mind. Something in me snapped; I saw Sneezy sitting on top of a table, walked over to him, and hit him with a straight right hand in the mouth. He reacted, grabbing at his mouth; he spat his incisor into his hand with blood.

"My hand was cut open from his tooth and gushing blood. When he came at me, I hit him with an institutional chair; they're plastic. By that time, the C.O.s came and broke it up. They took me to segregation and took Sneezy to the hospital. For several weeks, my open wound on my hand was constantly oozing a clear liquid from the cut, and I also broke my knuckle. I would learn later on that because the tooth was knocked out in tact, they were able to replace it in Sneezy's mouth.

"Shortly after that, I was picked up by Rob and Adam, the agents who always transported me. We took a twenty-minute drive to meet the federal marshals in a parking lot, and they handed me over. The marshals took me to the Witness Security Unit for my protection while serving my time.

WITSEC

In mid-April, 2017, the marshals took Borrello (Joey Russo) to a Witness Security Unit within driving distance of where he was being held. Once Borrello arrived, he was met by the unit manager. She presented Gene with a photo file of all the inmates to see if there was anyone with whom he may have had a problem.

Before Borrello could enter the unit, the population would look at his photo and sign a sheet, essentially saying there was no security threat. Right after he viewed the pictures, the unit manager gave Borrello the unit handbook and walked him through the Admission and Orientation process. All the rules were thoroughly explained.

During their conversation, the unit manager noticed Borrello's bandaged hand and asked what happened.

"I told her, 'I made a mistake.'

"She responded, 'Don't do that here. All these guys have murders.'

"When we finished our meeting, I was placed in a segregation cell for three days. It's standard operating procedure. Locked in on a Friday, and I was released Monday morning. At a WITSEC unit, you would think all the rooms would be single occupancy; not the case. You're initially placed in a double room with the guy who has the least seniority in the unit; as you earn more seniority, eventually you'll work your way into a single room.

"Released from segregation, I was put in a cell with a guy

whose case was out of the Eastern District of New York and who sentenced by Judge Ross, who gave him a harsh sentence for a guy who had worked undercover and worn a wire. This would be the judge to sentence me because she sentenced Uncle Vin. Once settled in, I began talking to the old-timers to learn how the Witness Protection Program worked. I learned there were only seven WITSEC or PC units throughout the United States. Two in New York, one in Florida, New Jersey, Pennsylvania, Arizona, and Minnesota. They were administered by the Federal Bureau of Prisons. But where there were security concerns, when the safety of a witness comes into question, the Office of Enforcement Operations would intervene. Everyone in the unit went by his initials and/or John Smith and his registration number.

"As I got familiar with more guys and began to let my guard down somewhat, some of the guys spoke more freely as well. You don't want to believe it, but when you have a Mafia case, it comes with resentment from your fellow inmates. The reason is simpl:, Mafia cases, especially cases where a low-level guy, a soldier, is cooperating against a highly publicized captain, he's gonna get a good deal. It's not so much what you give up, but who you give up. Or you give up so much information it cripples a Mafia family or organization. In the unit, there are Crips, Bloods, cartel members, terrorists, Latin Kings, MS13, Aryan Brotherhood, and Mafioso.

"As a person reared in a Mafia lifestyle, learning the rules of conduct, there was one thing I was proud of: we never hurt an innocent woman or child. The Mexican drug cartels and MS13 members kill innocents. They have no problem should you cooperate, as long as you don't tell on the cartel or the gang. Should you refuse to cooperate, they're killing your family, butchering them savagely. To the credit of the Mafia, their vendetta is with the individual.

"The Aryan Brotherhood and other white suprema cists groups cooperate on crimes that occur within the prison walls. Usually the cases are about murders in prison, but sometimes their reach from prison goes beyond the walls to the street. And there are oftentimes corrupt staff members who get sucked into their madness because of similar beliefs or sympathy.

"When after decades of treachery and killing or having inmates killed catches up with them, they tell, cooperate, and retire for the rest of their lives to these WITSEC units.

"The one thing I cannot wrap my head around is having to live with terrorists. Being from New York and living through the 9/11attack, I have a particular hatred for Najibullah Zazi. He was the terrorist who failed to detonate an explosive vest in the New York subway system. Fortunately for New York he was simply dumb. I would see the guy every day and have to bite my tongue and hold my hands, for I wanted to hit him.

"I know I'm a criminal. I made my own bed, but even for a criminal, there are limits. And lastly, just because I am a criminal, it does not mean I am any less patriotic.

"To lighten things up a little, I had come to find out the Howard Beach alumni who had been in the WITSEC unit. Joe Massino, 'Johnny Balls' Leto, Dave D'Arpino, Pete

Zuccaro, and Johnny Alite. Prior to cooperating, I had always wondered where these guys disappeared to. Now 1 know.

"When guys heard I was from New York, a guy named Nino approached me and asked, 'Where you from?'

"'Howard Beach.'

"'Oh, you know a Frank Nunziata? I was at GEO with him.'

"As soon as I heard Nunziata's name, I started laughing and responded, 'Yeah, that's the kid who put me in jail.'

"Nino told me Frank was in the unit in the GEO building that housed cooperators, telling everyone he wasn't a rat. The only way you get in is to cooperate. Everybody said he was scared to death in the GEO building. Could you imagine if he had had to go to Rikers Island?

"There were several high-profile witnesses in the unit when I was there. In fact, the first guy I met was Anthony Arillotta. He was a Genovese soldier working from Massachusetts who pleaded guilty in the killing of Adolfo Bruno, who was running Boston. Anthony was given the order to kill him by New York. When the deed was done, Anthony took over as acting boss. His co-defendant, 'Freddy Geese,' who didn't cooperate, was the guy who killed 'Whitey' Bulger, the notorious boss of the Summer Hill Gang in Boston. That's one thing, whether a witness unit or general population, it's a small world.

"Anthony had spoken well of Teddy Dipretoro and would introduce us; we would become very good friends.

"I would learn he had been in jail over thirty-five years for the bombing murder of the Philadelphia organized crime boss, Philip Testa. This guy cooperated from the outset. Completely debriefed, pleaded guilty to two murders, and provided information on the killing of two innocent guys. By 'innocent,' I mean not related to criminal activity, civilians. This guy does good time, helps people, got a college degree, and is a descent person. Knowing him, knowing what happened, I also know he should not be in prison.

"The next guy I would meet was Tony Angelo. He was with the Outfit out of Chicago, and he was working in Las Vegas during the late sixties and seventies. He was doing hits for the mob and was in Vegas during the time of the infamous mobster Tony Spilotro.

"Tony Angelo would become my barber. He had over forty years in prison, was a mean, nasty, old prick, but loved Donald Trump. Trump could do no wrong.

"I met a couple very high-level Mexican Cartel guys as well. Margarito 'Twin' Flores, by far one of the nicest guys I've met: generous, respectful, loved his wife and family, just a decent person. He was a high-level drug dealer and trafficker for the infamous 'El Chapo' Guzman of the Sinoloa Cartel. He will most likely be a key witness against El Chapo when he goes on trial in the United States.

"Frank Felix was one of the leaders of the extraordinarily violent Tijuana Cartel. But meeting him in the unit, he is a very friendly and humble guy. You would never know he wielded the power he once held. Very quiet, reserved, and respectful.

"The last of the high-profile guys I met was Joey 'Caves' Competiello, a Colombo soldier from Brooklyn who was under Dino Saracino. These guys were running Bensonhurst.

Nervous about the sentence I could receive, Joe put me at ease. He told me, 'Gene, I got six murders and killed a cop and got twelve years...you're gonna be okay.' With that I was put at ease that the government would give me a decent sentence.

THE NEXT CHAPTER

Gene Borrello cooperated with the federal government against Ronnie Giallanzo and the infamous mobster Vincent Asaro.

His release from prison in 2019 was due to his cooperation being deemed above average by a thoughtful and fair judge. In a way, Borrello saved himself from a life of treachery and violence or incarceration that would have taken his freedom from him until he was a senior citizen.

What will be the next steps in his life? One thing is certain: he can no longer return to life in the Mafia. If, somehow, he returns to a life of crime, it is clear that he will be returned to prison and likely die behind bars.

When Gene Borrello, at thirty-five years old, thinks about his future, his thoughts turn back to his years in the mob.

Make no mistake, my decisions were mine and mine alone; I make no excuses. There may be regrets, but those regrets are not born out of getting caught -they are real.

As a cooperating witness, there's no going back to the mob.

My life of crime is over.

As a kid, I was bad, disruptive in school, only went as far as the ninth grade, and got involved in crime at an early age. I was a teenager doing burglaries and selling drugs. If there was an opportunity to make fast money, you didn't have to ask me twice. Quite simply, I loved money, loved having money, and liked what money would buy.

As I got older and starting hanging out, being in my midteens, I began learning about the Mafia. One of my close friends would become Bobby G. A couple years later, I am around Ronnie G, his uncle, and the rest is history.

But I have learned a lot. Throughout this book, I have talked about crime, criminals, and my criminal acts. Now, as a mature man, I want to say how I see the mob and to close the book on that phase of my life.

In a word, the mob is treachery. Loan sharks want to lend, will gladly put the money in your hand and close your fist around the cash. Seven days later, you better have the vig. There is no excuse. The gangster will say, "I don't care. Fuck you, pay me." No payment? You will get a warning (verbal abuse). No money a second time, a beating. Try to stiff the loan shark, you will wind up hospitalized or dead.Sports books, as long as you are losing on the regular, you're good; win too much, you'll be conveniently robbed as soon as you get paid.

Throughout our society, the Mafia and Mafia life is overly glorified. In Italian enclaves throughout the country, but more so in the big cities, teenagers become enamored with the "life." The reality of living as a criminal among your Mafia brethren is quite different. Existence in the Mafia is a life of deceit, deception, manipulation, second guessing your friends, and every method of treachery conceivable. Then, when you are dealing with all that, you have to concern yourself with the feds. They're always coming. Once your name comes up, your days of freedom are counting down.

My greatest value to Ronnie G and Uncle Vin was my

willingness to act as their enforcer. Ronnie G and I were good friends, but I now know he wouldn't have been my friend had I not doled out beatings and shootings on his behalf.

I talk in this book about Bobby G being one of my closest friends. I was really disappointed in him when he left the "life" to become a working stiff and a civil servant, no less. Now, I realize he opted out of a life of treachery, betrayal, prison, and murder to live the life of a normal person. He knew something I didn't know.

At thirty-four years old, I've already spent a total of nine years in prison. The hardship of prison, beyond the obvious conditions, is loss. When the judge's gavel drops and that cell door slams shut, you lose everyone you love. This trip, I lost the woman I was in love with and would have made a life with. I have brothers that I don't know as well as I should because I missed so much of their lives. When your family is going through good times, you cannot be there to share the happiness, and when they're going through

bad times, you cannot be there to help because you are locked away far from home.

This time I cooperated. Because of this cooperation, there was an added cost. The guys I grew up with, social friends, are gone. While they weren't involved in the criminal life, they live in Howard Beach and cannot be known consorting with a known informant.

These were five or six guys I would have done anything for. We had been through many years of fun: partying, clowning, living, fighting, and more. I would have risked my life for any one of them. Having to leave these guys in my past hurts more than I can say.

"Looking ahead, my future is bright because I'll be free. Beyond that, it's a blur. Right now, I have more questions than answers.

"The government's Witness Protection Program is s not for me. Taking Phase II of the program would be more of a hindrance than a help" having to answer to marshals, explain myself...I'm done answering to authority. As far as my safety goes, I never gave it a second thought. I was the guy who, when sent, struck fear in the heart of the victim. Many of the victims were criminals themselves. Had I not provided information against Ronnie G and Uncle Vin, the government would have been trying to put me away for life for my violent past, for I was the bad guy. I will not be hanging out on Crossbay Boulevard, Mafia central, but I will not be hiding, either.

"I am at my wit's end trying to explain my future to you. Basically, I am attempting to explain the future when no one knows what the future holds. There is one certainty: I will not be going back to prison. So my future, like most people's, lies somewhere between the unknown and known. I have no doubt I will find my way."

BONUS STORY
Lufthansa Heist

"The Lufthansa Heist, as it became commonly known, made headline news across the country. It rose to prominence for its daringness and infamy and would not be forgotten for decades. It was a high-profile robbery of millions of dollars of cash and jewelry during 1978. The investigative onslaught spurred by the crime would raise paranoia to untenable levels...bodies started to drop.

"Interestingly, when the formulation of the plan was being hatched, the robbery crew was not to be Mafioso. The Mafia got involved because the first robbery crew backed out. My guess is that it was too big, would generate too much heat, and there was fear of eventual arrest.

"A robbery of that magnitude requires inside information, someone in the know with a weakness or larceny in their heart. There was such a person, Louis Werner, a Lufthansa employee with the needed access and procedural knowledge to make the crime doable. Not only had Werner provided information a couple years earlier, he had a trial run. Werner was first employed by Lufthansa in 1968. At some point, he became responsible for all cargo identified as 'IMPORTANT' or 'VALUABLE.' Any cargo identified as such was locked and sealed. On flight 493, which arrived at JFK Airport on October 8th, Werner had to remove bags containing foreign currency. When he entered the plane, he claimed he had diarrhea and abruptly left the plane. Shortly thereafter, he returned, but before he could remove any cargo again, he abruptly left with diarrhea.

"Within fifteen minutes, Werner returned to remove one or more bags identified as valuable containing foreign currency. He was to secure the bags in the cargo building.

"The bag containing the foreign currencies never made it to the cargo building. Somehow, it was inadvertently picked up by another cargo-handling company working for Lufthansa. When the employee realized he mistakenly picked up the bag, he returned the bag to its shipping container located outside the cargo building. A short while later, when the midnight crew arrived, they took in the containers. The freight handlers performed an inventory and found foreign currencies missing, valued at twenty-two thousand American dollars.

"Werner had stolen the money. Concerned he would be found out, the following day, he left the money with his friend and coworker, Peter Gruenewald. They agreed further that Pete would convert the currency to American dollars. But after nearly a couple of weeks, Pete never converted the cash. Werner retrieved the money and gave it to William Fischetti, who achieved the currency conversion by year's end.

"Lufthansa performed a cursory investigation. The amount was not significant, and the money was insured. Louis Werner skirted suspicion, maintained his job handling and securing important and valuable cargo.

"Louis was a patient man. He got a taste of ill-gotten gains. He was in a position to bide his time and wait for a bigger score. Little did Louis know, a couple of years later, that would be one of the most infamous robberies in history, known to the public as the Lufthansa Heist.

"Louis was anxious for a bigger score. Meeting with his friends, Peter Gruenewald and William Fischetti agreed they would have to assemble a robbery crew.

"Gruenewald believed he had friends who would be willing to do the eventual stick-up. With the lure of big money in the air, they were 'in.' But when, as time passed and the 'big score' didn't materialize as quickly as expected, they bailed. With no crew available, Pete and Bill wanted to do a smaller robbery or theft from Lufthansa, but Louis had dreams of big money from a big robbery.

"With Gruenewald and Fischetti out of the picture, Louis would move on. He chose to ask his bookmaker, Frankie Menna, if he knew anybody. Werner knew he had ties to the underworld and would be able to put him in touch with the right people. Sure enough, as soon as Werner floated the idea, Menna had a guy. He put him in touch with Martin 'Marty' Krugman, who was absolutely interested.

"Marty either got architectural plans or constructed his own plans of the Lufthansa terminal. My guess is he sat down with Werner, since he worked there, and constructed a top view drawing of the area.

"With plans in hand and an opportunity for a 'big score,' Marty had no problem convincing Jimmy 'The Gent' Burke of doing the job. Burke got the nickname 'The Gent' because he always left the drivers with cash for their trouble. The Gent was a thief and armed robber and the right guy for the job.

"Jimmy was also a notoriously dangerous gangster and a dear friend to Uncle Vin.

"Burke had told Krugman that he had assembled a robbery team -they were on standby waiting for the right opportunity.

Marty was a hyperactive person with no patience. He was relentlessly bothering Burke about carrying out the robbery. Little did Krugman know, Burke was waiting for the go-ahead from their inside guy, Louis Werner. Burke was no dummy; he was a seasoned criminal. He was waiting until there was a greater chance of a big payday. He wanted to get the odds in his favor. Time was on his side. But then there was fuckin' Marty.

"When the cargo arrived on the plane, there was no way of knowing the exact contents. One could venture a guess of value based on the delivery address and the manifest identifying the items as important or valuable. At the end of the day, one was making an educated guess. Louis Werner made that educated guess on Friday, December 8, 1978.

"A Brinks armored car arrived at the Lufthansa cargo area to pick up packages for Chase Manhattan Bank. This was the shipment Werner wanted. Normally, Werner would have assigned Lufthansa employees to deliver the cargo of currency, but this time, he did not. Instead, when the Brinks truck arrived, Werner told the armored car guys he couldn't release the shipment. The guards demanded their shipment from Werner. He would not release the shipment without the presence of a supervisor or security officer. Werner had implemented a new procedure on his own.

"The Brinks guards remained at the terminal. Werner bided his time. Eventually, the guards could wait no longer; they had other pick-ups and deliveries to make, so they left.

"Werner would finish his shift and put the plan into action. "Werner made the call. Burke snapped into action, rounding up all his guys and telling them to be ready. Time was on their side; the shipment would remain secured in the terminal until Monday. They had all weekend to figure out exactly the best time to make their move. It was determined they would strike Monday, December 11th, in the wee hours of the morning. Jimmy 'The Gent' was calling the shots; this was his operation. When it came to crime, he was like a conductor leading an orchestra.

"The robbery crew descended upon the Lufthansa cargo terminal at three o'clock Monday morning. Six masked men, guns drawn, caught the employees on their break in the break room.

When they heard, 'Nobody move,' the Lufthansa employees were in shock, frozen and quickly overwhelmed. One thief ordered one of the employees to deactivate the alarm system; the employee readily complied. The robbery team threatened to shoot unless everyone complied. Their objective was not to hurt anyone; by convincing the employees they were serious and dangerous actually made it safer for the workers. The next order barked was demanding access to the area or room where valuables were stored. The holdup men took forty boxes containing jewelry and cash, loading them in a black van.

"The driver of the van was a black guy called 'Stacks,' and driving the crash car was Gasper Valenti, Uncle Vin's cousin. Uncle Vin made sure he had someone there to represent and protect his interest.

"John F. Kennedy Airport was territory shared by Paul Varrio (Luchese) and Uncle Vin. Any criminal activity that occurred in that area by an affiliate or Mafioso, Uncle Vin was supposed to get a cut. If a guy held out or insultingly shorted Uncle Vin on his end, a beating, shooting, or killing would ensue. In addition to Gasper, Jimmy Burke was a close friend to Uncle Vin. Gasper was Uncle Vin's eyes and ears on scene, for what Uncle Vin don't know, he couldn't lay claim to. There is some truth to that adage, 'There is no honor among thieves.'

"The van was offloaded, the boxes put in the chase car and Jimmy Burkes's car. They went to a prearranged garage to unload the haul. Gasper remained with Jimmy; they took a quick count of the loot, and Gasper headed to see Uncle Vin. My guess is that Jimmy would divide the take later. The haul was safe and secure for the time being.

"Late that day, the news coverage would rank the Lufthansa Heist as the largest armed robbery in United States history. Even though the crime would be solved, neither the jewelry nor the cash would ever be retrieved. The links to the robbers would be severed. There would be no prosecutable evidence; only hearsay evidence to a level of 'he said, she said.' Amongst federal prosecutors in New York, this was a trophy case because of its high profile status and involved Mafia membership. It checked two boxes; the Assistant United States Attorney who got the conviction, his career would be made.

"When Jimmy got a count of the money, there would be five million in United States dollars and nearly one million in jewelry. Uncle Vin, being a friend of Burke, and it being his shared territory, received eighty hundred thousand dollars from the infamous Lufthansa Heist.

"Louis Werner, the inside guy, for his idea and assistance, was supposed to be paid three hundred thousand. Of which, he had promised Peter Gruenewald sixty-five thousand to keep quiet, but eventually Werner would give Gruenewald ten thousand. It was not enough to keep him quiet.

"Louis Werner was arrested in March of 1979. The friends he initially sought help from would line up against him. Peter Gruenewald and William Fischetti would debrief and testify at Werner's trial. Louis would be found guilty and sentenced to fifteen years in a federal institution.

"With Werner going on trial, two witnesses against him, the robbers were not paid their full share because Jimmy was getting nervous. But worst of all, Marty Krugman kept breaking Jimmy's balls; he wanted more money -they all did. Marty should have known better.

"Jimmy 'The Gent' was not only a notorious thief, he was also a notorious killer. Street lore credits him with murders going back to when he was a teenager.

"Throughout his life, there would be many more that he would kill or order killed. Jimmy was the highest-level mob associate with the Luchese crime family. Uncle Vin said that had Jimmy been Italian, he would have been a boss. The situation and paranoia got the better of him, and bodies started dropping. Jimmy either personally killed or ordered to be killed everyone who had ties to the Lufthansa Heist. Not only did Jimmy sever the riskiest ties to The Heist, he also didn't have to pay their full share; they were dead. Marty Krugman, Joe 'Buddha' Manri, Robert 'Frenchy' McMahon, and Tommy DeSimone were off the count. Gasper Valenti got a pass because he was related to Uncle Vin.

"Based on what Uncle Vin had told me, four guys received money from the robbery: Paul Varrio (Burke's captain), Jimmy Burke, and Uncle Vin.

"Over thirty-five years later, another case would be tried by the federal government related to the Lufthansa robbery and related murders. In United States v. Vincent Asaro, 2015 U.S. Dist. LEXIS 137002 (E.D.N.Y. 2015), the government would try Uncle Vin at the age of eighty for the 1978 Lufthansa jewelry heist and related murders. The trial would be awash with 'credible informants' (CIs) and "'confidential witnesses' (CW's). Each had been assigned a number into the double digits, there were so many.

"Uncle Vin was charged with robbery, extortion, and RICO; the government wanted their pound of flesh. They used Credible Witness number 5, or Anthony 'Fat Andy' Ruggiano, son of one of Vin's closest friends and an infamous Gambino captain. One interesting fact: Anthony would testify that his father confessed to him that one year after The Heist, Asaro and Burke conspired with him to fence the jewelry. Fat Andy speculated to his son that the reason they wanted to fence the jewelry with him was so they would not have to kick money to their Bonanno and Luchese superiors.

"Uncle Vin's cousin, Gasper Valenti, wore a wire on Uncle Vin for three years. A couple of the highlights of Gasper's information was Uncle Vin explaining how he killed Pete Katz in 1969 by strangling him with a dog chain, then buried the body in Burke's basement.

"Uncle Vin rambled on incessantly to Gasper, causing all of his codefendants to accept plea deals. Vin would call the boss, Tommy DiFiore, the fat herb from Long Island. And he would go on and on.

"Nicole Argentieri, the Assistant United States Attorney prosecuting the case, specialized in organized crime cases; specifically, Bonanno cases. Nicole was an authoritative and brilliant lawyer. In the government's eyes, the conviction of Uncle Vin was a foregone conclusion. They had three years of wiretaps. Vin never took the stand. His lawyer argued quite simply that not one witness can place him at the scene of any crime.

"For reasons unbeknownst to anyone, when the parties rested and the case went to the jury, Uncle Vin was acquitted and walked free. Nicole was upset to the point where she physically trembled. The headlines of one of the newspapers read, 'The Jolly Fella.'

"The government was not done with Uncle Vin, not by a long shot. Nicole had planned to take a well-paying job in the private sector after the Asaro trial. She wanted to conclude her government service on a high note. She would remain in government service as an Assistant United States Attorney while managing several law offices in the private sector. She would make one last push at Asaro. I was in jail, facing the next thirty years of my life behind bars. Witnesses were lining up against me; guys were debriefing. I was dead, and the government knew it. Unfortunately, I knew it as well."

AND NOW WHAT?

Throughout the writing of this book, through the many in-person meetings, lengthy telephone interviews, and hundreds of texts and e-mails, Gene Borrello was a perfect gentleman. The author did know that Borrello, at times, would show some anger when he explained certain stories where he was upset or perceived he was being screwed somehow.

Borrello was indeed the perfect gentlemen, especially when it came to discussing his various girlfriends and love interests. Not once did he show disrespect or kiss-and-tell, as so many young men do with their ex-paramours. Gene was more than evasive when the author asked him questions about his women to spice things up a bit in the book. Gene ignored the questions or changed the subject, never getting into the sexy stuff that helps sell books and that movie producers tend to love.

Borrello was especially guarded when asked about former girlfriend Samantha Gaudino, protecting her reputation as a Doberman guards his master's home.

"She was a very good person. A really nice person." Is the most Gene would comment on Sam.

Gene had a lot going for him since he returned from prison. Staying away from the mob and its trappings was likely the biggest thing for Gene. He knew that "the life" was left behind and all bridges were burned. "The Johnny and Gene Show" with John Alite, the former Gambino enforcer, had tens of thousands of followers and viewers and Gene was fast becoming a celebrity.

Gene's story would soon be available in a book and there were several producers who were interested in making a series or a feature film. Above all, Gene was happy being out of prison and home with his family and friends.

Deep down, however, Gene was still Gene.

So, it was a great shock to many people, and not such an amazement to others, to pick up the New York Post on February 2, 2021 and see Gene's mugshot, front and center, in the tabloid.

Borrello had called Samantha on January 24th of that year to ask her permission to use a photo of him and her together from their dating years in his book. He didn't need her permission to use the shot, but he called her, nonetheless. Maybe he wanted to show respect to his former girlfriend, maybe he wanted to speak with the now married Samantha, or maybe he just wanted to let her know there was a book coming out about his life. Only Gene's deep-down honesty could reveal his motivation.

The communication backfired big time. Borrello asked his former girlfriend to use the photograph and she went ballistic on him, attacking him like a pit bull.

"You need to get checked. You need to think about who the fuck you are." Sam replied.

Her comments triggered Gene's famous temper.

The argument continued with Samantha threatening to call the police during their call.

According to published reports, 'Assistant US Attorney

Lindsay Gerdes recounted the exchange in a Brooklyn federal court at the Monday bail hearing: Referring to Borrello Gerdes said: "He said, 'The minute you call the cops on me and grow those balls, you watch, I'll blow your husband's head right off in the middle of the street. Remember what I used to do. I will grab your father right now and beat the dog shit out of him. Be happy I don't grab you and your fat, ugly husband by the neck and drag you down the street,'" Gerdes continued. "Gene had left messages to Samantha on voice notes."

Borello was also arrested for his association with convicted mafia member John Alite on their YouTube show, "The Johnny and Gene Show." He also appeared on several episodes of Alite's podcast "KONCRETE" — which Gerdes said "effectively glorifies crime and that type of activity committed by the La Cosa Nostra."

The newspaper report continued: "Alite has stated numerous times on their YouTube channel that they in no way intend to glorify the mafia life but are rather trying to save kids from entering the 'life of treachery.'"

In court, Gene pleaded with the Assistant US Attorney, "I don't know why you're doing this to me, Lindsay? I made one mistake with my ex-girlfriend, why are you burying me like this?"

According to Borrello, there is an interesting backstory. It seems that Gene and Samantha, through the young woman's mother made up and all was forgiven.

Two weeks after the incident, Gene, thinking the incident was forgiven and forgotten, received a call from a well-known reporter of mob news.

The reporter informed Gene that he had heard Borrello was going to jail for having violated his parole with the threats he had leveled at Samantha.

According to Borrello, Samantha called him to say it wasn't her but her husband Rob who had taken the steps to pursue charges.

Shortly after the call from the reporter, Gene was seen entering a Wendy's fast-food restaurant in Woodhaven, Queens by New York State Police on a registration check. Gene was informed there was a warrant for parole violation out on him and he was arrested and taken to a local NYPD precinct.

Gene was soon sent to MDC Brooklyn Detention Center and faced Judge Hale, who informed him that he was being remanded as a public risk and a threat to the community. Borrello was sent to the East Shu house within MDC for sixty-two days in solitary confinement. He was then sent to another house within the jail for another sixty days with other inmates.

Most of the inmates knew about Gene's reputation in the Bonnano family and his recent parole violation from the newspapers.

Why it took so long after the threats made to Samantha for Gene's arrest is a matter of conjecture. It seems that Sam's husband is friendly with a mafia made man by the name of Pudgy and another mob associate, Anthony Conza.

Coincidently, there were several people making a

mockery of Borrello in internet chats, and many phone calls were being made to the District Attorney's office residents of Howard Beach Queens and other locations nearby, all excoriating Borrello.

Ironically, Borrello and Conza were good friends at one time.

According to Borrello, Conza's wife had a relationship with Gene's friend and associate, Mike Palmaccio, who hooked her on heroin and prostituted her. The young woman died of a heroin overdose. This could have been the reason why Conza was seeking to hurt Gene and helped to have him violated. Again, this is supposition, and there are no facts to support this theory.

After his time at MDC, Borrello was facing a five-year bit in State Prison for violating his parole. Instead, the prosecutor settled for a one-year parole with the following stipulations:
• No visiting Howard Beach
• No association with ex-convicts or mob members
• No use of social media, including podcasts
• No contact with Samantha
• Weekly anger management sessions

Will Borrello keep his nose clean and stick with the court's stipulations?

Gene undoubtedly has anger issues. It will take professional psychologists to help him deal with his hair-trigger anger. They will need to get to the root cause of his temper flare ups and give him the coping tools that he will need to keep Gene from using his explosive rage going forward in his still very young life.

Above all, Gene is not stupid. He will stay on the straight and narrow and use this experience as a building block for a better, more fruitful life.

1. Gene's grandfather, a Korean War veteran. 2. Gene and his grandmother. 3. Gene (second from left) and friends. 4. Gene, Ronnie G., and his family. 5. Maria and Gene, 2005.

1. Gene (center) and friends. 2. Bobby G. and Gene at Club Posh, Long Island. 3. Gene (second from left) and friends. 4. Bobby G. and Gene

This page: Photos taken during time at Metropolitan Detention Center, Brooklyn (MDC Brooklyn)

1. Samantha and Gene in Miami.
2. Gene and Frankie Pasqua, 2008.
3. Gene (center) and friends.

1. Gene's grandfather, uncle Joe, and cousin Anthony.
2. John Gotti and Gene, 2012. 3. Samantha and Gene,
2013.